THE DOCTOR AND THE DEVILS

This dramatic story, written in the form of a film scenario, is based on the case of the murderers Burke and Hare which came to trial in Edinburgh more than a hundred years ago. It centres round the figure of Thomas Rock, a lecturer in anatomy, and the body-snatchers who supply corpses for medical theatres. It is a grim subject, to which the author brings a poetic quality, both in the dialogue spoken by the diverse male and female characters and in the 'film shooting directions.'

By Dylan Thomas

COLLECTED POEMS, 1934–1952

DEATHS AND ENTRANCES
  Poems

PORTRAIT OF THE ARTIST AS A
                    YOUNG DOG
  Fictional autobiography

UNDER MILK WOOD
  A play for voices

THE DOCTOR AND THE DEVILS
  A film scenario

QUITE EARLY ONE MORNING
  Broadcasts

A PROSPECT OF THE SEA
  Stories and prose writings
      (Summer 1955)

THE DOCTOR
AND THE DEVILS

by

DYLAN THOMAS

from the story by

DONALD TAYLOR

LONDON
J. M. DENT & SONS LTD

All rights reserved
Made in Great Britain
at the
Aldine Press · Letchworth · Herts
for
J. M. DENT & SONS LTD
Aldine House · Bedford Street · London
First published 1953
Last reprinted 1962

*An account by Donald Taylor of the origin of this film scenario,
and of the historical facts and characters on which it is based, is printed
on page 135 at the end of this volume.*

THE DOCTOR AND THE DEVILS

I

Music.

From a long way off, we see a deserted road winding downwards
from a hill-top.

Huge sky, slow clouds.

A small black figure appears at the top of the road, and moves
downhill. A small black figure with another darkness billowing
around it.

Now we see the downhill-approaching figure as a top-hatted man in
the wind. From our distance he is still the mystery of a man,
alone in a blowing morning on a lonely hill-top; still the shadow,
not the recognizably featured substance, of a man.

Closer now, we see that he is a youngish man in severe professional
black; and his long cloak is the other darkness around him.

Closer still, we see his body and face as he strides down towards us.
He wields his stick like a prophet's staff. We see the deep-set eyes
behind the large spectacles; the wide sensual mouth tightened into
its own denial; the wild fringes of hair blowing from under the
sides of the stiff hat-rim; the coffin-shaped forehead; the in-
satiable, and even predatory, curiosity of the bent-forward head.

Suddenly he stops, looks down.

Now, with his eyes, we see the City that lies below him. An early
nineteenth-century City, its crossing, twisting patterns of roofs at so
many different levels, its streets and houses dangerously clambering,
scaling, falling down from the steep hill, its patchwork of threading
alleys, its compact wilderness of little archwayed courts and closes,
sunless dead ends, market spaces surrounded by tumbling top-
heavy tenements, hovels, cottages, pigsties . . .

I

And now, from behind him, we see him stride on, top-hat and stick, towards the City; towards the rising sigh of city sounds, the mingling and slowly loudening voices of people and bells, the noise of hooves and wheels on cobble stones, and street cries unintelligibly distant.

DISSOLVE to

2

CITY MARKET-PLACE.

And up come the City sounds.

The straw-strewn cobbles of the Market are crowded with stalls. Stalls that sell rags and bones, kept by rags and bones. Stalls that sell odds and ends of every odd kind, odd boots, bits of old meat, fish heads, trinkets, hats with feathers, broadsheets, hammers. Stalls with shawls. Stalls like ash bins. Anything that is market-able, to the very poor.

Pigs and chickens grunt, root, cluck, and peck among the straw heaps and the refuse, getting in every one's way though no one notices or cares.

A heaped high hay-cart rumbles over the cobbles.

The doors of the shops and the public-houses are open on to the Market, and singing comes from inside some of them, and outside some of them stand men and women drinking.

And men and women lean, drinking, against the stalls.

There are many, many children, some very old.

Among the children, the butt of their noise, is a humpback with the smile of an idiot.

And across the Market the man in cloak and top-hat is walking: black and purposeful among all the turbulent laziness, among the talkers, the hawkers, the old leaners, the drinkers, the shrill children.

We move with him.

Two men whom we see we will remember later. With earthenware tankards in their hands, they are standing almost in the middle of the Market. One is tall and very thin; the other squat, barrel-chested. The tall one is hollow-cheeked, corpse-pale, with jerky,

2

inconsequent gestures; the short one full and ruddy-faced, knob-nosed, surly, slow-moving.

We see that the tall one is laughing: at nothing. We hear his laugh: a high-pitched snarl, an animal noise. The squat one pays no attention, but curses the whole Market with his scowling eyes.

We see a woman pushing a barrow heaped with rags and hucksters' scraps, and another woman trailing behind her.

We hear the first woman's cry as she turns into a side alley:

> Rags and bones . . . rags and bones . . .

she cries.

And then the cry of the second woman:

> . . . Cat-skin . . . human hair . . .

The faces of the two women also we shall remember.

> Rags, rags . . . rags and bones . . .
> Cat-skin . . . human hair . . .

The tall man mimics the cries.

A hawker passes, crying her cry of:

> Fresh herrings . . . fresh herrings . . .

We hear behind her cry the high yelping mimicry of the tall drinker.

The man in cloak and top-hat moves on.

And the noises of the Market fade as we

DISSOLVE to

3

CITY SQUARE.

The man in cloak and top-hat is walking through the trimly treed garden in the Square towards a large building.

We follow him into the building.

4

HALLWAY OF ROCK'S ACADEMY.

As he walks through the Hallway, a Porter, in black coat, black trousers, and brass-buttoned waistcoat, approaches him. He is a little man with a very pale face.

3

PORTER. They're here, Doctor Rock.

Rock stops.

>ROCK. Indeed, Mr. Forsythe? Who or what are 'they,' and where is 'here'?
>
>PORTER. The specimens for the Anatomical Museum, sir, are in the Museum.
>
>ROCK. How fortunate they are not in the gentlemen's cloak-room. I should hate skeletons in all my cupboards. Thank you.

Rock walks to the end of the Hallway, opens a door, goes through.

5

SMALL CLOAK-ROOM.

Rock hangs up his hat and cloak, very neatly, puts his stick in a stand, and turns to look at himself in a full-length mirror.

We see, in the mirror, that he is wearing a long, dark coat, immaculately tailored, an ornate, embroidered waistcoat across which gold chains hang in festoons, a high cravat, higher than is the fashion of the gentlemen we shall see in future scenes, with its folds passed through a diamond ring, a prominent shirt-collar, delicately plaited cambrics, watch-seals and pendants, dark trousers, shining boots, a gay waist-band.

At all this excellence he looks with approval; he preens himself, he flicks off invisible dust.

Softly he says to his reflection:

>ROCK. Well, Thomas. To work!

And he crosses the Cloak-room to another door, and opens it, and walks through.

From the Cloak-room door we see into:

6

THE ANATOMICAL MUSEUM.

It is a very large room.

Around the walls are anatomical specimens mounted and labelled.

4

There are specimens in glass cases, many unmounted specimens, and a great number of packing-cases of all sizes.

Assistants are unpacking the cases.

All over the floor are bones; the skeletons of birds, beasts, reptiles, fishes; odd fish; fossils; osteological curiosities; pickled monsters; brains in jars; the scattered treasures of a static, silent zoo.

Rock, some distance from his assistants, is opening a case and throwing aside the top layers of straw.

We TRACK TOWARDS him.

He takes a little skeleton from the case: the skeleton of a baby or a monkey.

A man's voice is heard.

> MAN'S VOICE. Good Morning, Thomas.

Rock looks round.

PAN ROUND to door through which a heavily built, elderly man is entering. His hair is close clipped and iron grey, his demeanour severe, his face unaccustomed to smiling.

Now, from the door, we see him cross over to Rock.

They shake hands.

Rock still holds the little skeleton under one arm.

> ROCK. Doctor Manson! You see me to-day, sir, with one foot in the grave. Now, where is a chair?

He looks around the Museum room.

> ROCK. Perhaps you could make yourself comfortable on this case of . . .

He glances at a label on a packing-case near him.

> ROCK. . . . stomachs of cetacea. I am *sure* there was a chair here yesterday. I remember it distinctly . . .
>
> MANSON. You probably talked its hind legs off. Don't fuss around me, Thomas. I shall sit here on your stomachs.

Manson sits on the near case.

Rock puts the little skeleton carefully down. He goes on unpacking specimens throughout the conversation.

MANSON. You look well. Odd, but well. How is your wife?

ROCK. Well, and not at all odd, thank you, sir. Oh, the doctors' wives still cut her in the street, but fortunately they resemble their husbands at an operation: they cannot cut anything properly. And you, sir?

MANSON. I am an old man. You should not ask old men how they feel, or they will tell you. I am old, like Doctor Hocking.

ROCK. Doctor Hocking was in his second childhood before he was adolescent. When he is your age, sir—a good age —he'll be old as the grandfather of a tortoise, take a week to put his boots on, a fortnight to suck his bread and milk, and a month to make up his absence of mind.

MANSON. You still do not approve of the distinguished Professor of Anatomy in our University.

ROCK. I still do not approve of stupidity and inefficiency, and sycophantic compromise, and pretentious, intolerable airs and graces.

MANSON. [Unsmiling, as throughout.] You speak too highly of him.

ROCK. He has become a professor on no wits at all. If he were a half-wit, with *his* self-assertion he would be known as a Scotch Sophocles.

MANSON. I am thinking of retiring, Thomas.

ROCK. If you leave your School of Anatomy, sir, you consign the medical reputation of the City to a man who reads his grandfather's lectures for his own and dissects like a labourer with a pick.

MANSON. I have no intention of leaving my students to *Doctor Hocking*. I would rather continue lecturing myself, toothless, on crutches, with my beard to my boots. I founded *my* School to keep the teaching of Anatomy away from hacks and drudges and medical impostors, crammers, and quacks. [Slowly, emphatically.] My successor must be a person of precision, method, vigilance, and expertness.

6

ROCK. In this City?

MANSON. I have found him.

ROCK. Oh, in heaven, sir, not here.

MANSON. In a museum.

ROCK. In a mummy-case?

MANSON. No, standing like a fool in front of me, with a leg
under his arm.

Manson looks at Rock. And from his eyes we see Rock standing,
a plaster leg under his arm, among the specimens he has unpacked
from the cases; Rock staring back at Manson.

And we *TRACK BACK* to see Rock and Manson still, silent, in
the great room surrounded by bones and bodies, like men in a
spilt graveyard.

DISSOLVE to

7

A ROOM IN ROCK'S HOUSE (henceforward to be known as ELIZA-
BETH'S ROOM).

It is an intimate, comfortable room.

A fire is blazing in the deep fire-place.

There is a table with sewing upon it.

And another small table with books.

Rock stands at the long window of the room, looking out.

Coming closer to him, we see, through the window, the roofs of
the City.

It is dusk in autumn.

A woman comes in. She is young, small, fair, with a candid,
tranquil face.

She is carrying a tray with biscuits and a glass of milk on it.

She stands for a moment, looking at Rock.

Then he turns.

ROCK. I never heard you come in, Elizabeth. You're a witch

7

in a white apron. Downstairs you keep a little instrument, no bigger than a baby mouse, that can hear my brain ticking and my heart beating.

Elizabeth puts the tray down on a table.

ROCK. [Gently.] Shall I tell you my news now? Or shall I kiss you first . . .

Elizabeth smiles calmly up at him.

ELIZABETH. Yes.

He kisses her.

ROCK. . . . and ask you what you have been doing all day . . .

ELIZABETH. Oh, the ordinary things.

ROCK. . . . and how our little boy behaved . . .

ELIZABETH. He's asleep now. He said his prayers, and then he said there was a tiger in his bed.

She smiles.

ELIZABETH. Tell me your news now.

ROCK. Do you remember Doctor Manson? Stern as a judge and solid as a mountain. When I was a student, he had the bearing and the voice of a god surrounded by the angels of logic.

Now he's old, and ill. He knows death. He can hear it growling and scratching around him now, like a dog after a bone.

He wants me to take his place. Do you know what that means? A whole School of Anatomy outside any influence but Manson's and my own. All the work I have ever wanted to do, I can do there. Can you see me as another St. Hilaire, my dear, another Cuvier? . . . Another old stick-in-the-mud, maybe, with bees in his bald head . . .

The room is growing slowly darker.

ROCK. I said 'Yes' to Manson. Are you glad?

Elizabeth nods.

> ROCK. When one burns one's boats, what a very nice fire it makes.

He looks out of the window, over the roofs in the gathering darkness, Elizabeth near him. He speaks almost as though to himself alone.

> ROCK. What can spoil or hurt us now? Nothing, nothing, nothing. Nothing out there. . . .

He makes a gesture towards the dusky City.

> ROCK. My future 's here.

He raises his hands, palms upwards, then draws them back towards him, inviting Elizabeth.

She moves to him, and he takes her hands.

> ROCK. And some of it is in your hands. Oh, I am happy to-day, Elizabeth, happy and tired.
> I am tired of the dead! . . .

He puts his arm around her, draws her close. Together they stand at the window. His hand moves along her bare arm.

FADE OUT.

FADE IN

8

LECTURE HALL OF ROCK'S ACADEMY.

Rock is on the platform, lecturing.

Another younger man sits at a small table on the other side of the platform.

The amphitheatre is crowded with students.

Rock, as a lecturer, shows a rare felicity of movement, now reminding us of the slow and graceful minuet, then the quiet pose or soldierly *attention*; and these again are succeeded by the rapid gesture. After each diversion of his subject he readjusts his spectacles, draws up his gay waist-band and then, presenting a steady front to his class, resumes his prelection.

ROCK. I stand before you, gentlemen, as a lecturer in Anatomy, a scientist, a specialist, a *material* man to whom the heart, for instance, is an elaborate physical organ and not the 'seat of love,' a man to whom the 'soul,' because it has no shape, does not exist.

But paradox is inherent in all dogma, and so I stand before you also as a man of sentiment, of spiritual aspirations, intellectually creative impulses, social convictions, moral passions. And it is in my dual capacity of scientist and sociologist, materialist and moralist, anatomist and artist, that I shall attempt to conduct my lectures, to expound, inform, illustrate, entertain, and edify.

Our aim for ever must be the pursuit of the knowledge of Man in his entirety. To study the flesh, the skin, the bones, the organs, the nerves of Man, is to equip our minds with a knowledge that will enable us to search *beyond* the body. The noble profession at whose threshold you stand as neophytes is not an end in itself. The science of Anatomy contributes to the great sum of all Knowledge, which is the Truth: the whole Truth of the Life of Man upon this turning earth. And so: Observe precisely. Record exactly. Neglect nothing. Fear no foe. Never swerve from your purpose. Pay no heed to Safety.

For I believe that all men can be happy and that the good life can be led upon this earth.

I believe that all men must work towards that end.

And I believe that that end justifies any means. . . .

Let no scruples stand in the way of the progress of medical science!

Rock bows: a curt, but studied bow.

The students rise.

And Rock walks off the platform.

The other man on the platform makes a gesture of dismissal to the students, then follows Rock.

And all the students suddenly begin talking as they move down the Lecture Hall.

9

HALLWAY OF ROCK'S ACADEMY.

Rock and his companion on the platform are walking through the
Hallway towards a door under the stairs. They open the door
and go through. We follow them, through the open door, into a

10

SMALL CLOAK-ROOM.

It is a bare, dark room. A few pegs on the wall—Rock's cloak and
top-hat hang from one—and a table with a water jug and a
basin on it.

Rock rolls up his sleeves, very circumspectly, as his companion
pours water into the basin.

We hear, from outside, the noise of the students.

> ROCK. [With a nod towards the noise.] What do they talk
> about afterwards, I wonder? Do they repeat one's words
> of golden guidance? Or make disparaging remarks about
> one's waistcoat? I think when I was a student we used
> to tell one another stories: they were anatomical, too. Ah,
> thank you, Murray. . . .

Rock begins to wash his hands in the basin. Murray takes off his
coat.

> MURRAY. You agree with all you said?
> ROCK. But naturally.
> MURRAY. 'The end justifies *any* means'? That is—to say
> the least of it—unscrupulous.
> ROCK. Then do not say 'the least of it.' Say 'the most':
> that it is *honest*.

And Murray begins to wash his hands.

> ROCK. You're coming to my dinner, of course? I can

guarantee the cooking. Only the conversation will be half-baked and only the politeness overdone.

MURRAY. [Smiling.] Of course . . .

ROCK. . . . Do not trust an elder sister to choose one's company for one. Annabella will never believe I am properly grown up and so sits me down next to an elderly lady whose conversational ability would disgrace a defective three-year-old, or else closets me with a deaf historian so far advanced into the next world that he can only dribble and splutter in this.

MURRAY. [With a kind of tolerant affection.] Dinner will be a monologue, as usual, Thomas. I can't think how you ever manage to eat or drink anything at all on those occasions. . . .

ROCK. I eat during the yawns.

Now he has finished washing. He adjusts his coat-sleeves. And Murray helps him on with his cloak.

ROCK. I *loathe* all Dinners with a capital 'D.' Why can't I have a *quiet* meal with a small 'm' and a large port?

MURRAY. Oh, but William! A Dinner to Celebrate the Opening of the New Session of Doctor Rock's Academy!

ROCK. I wish it were still Rock's and Manson's Academy . . .

He puts on his top-hat. Murray passes him his stick.

ROCK. [As though to himself.] . . . Poor Manson . . . [Suddenly in a different mood.] If Annabella hasn't invited at least one Duke I shall be so surprised that I shall have to ask one myself. And throw in a drunk baronet for bad measure.

Good night, Murray.

He walks to the door of the small, dark room.

MURRAY. Good night. Sleep well.

ROCK. Don't be a dam' fool. . . .

Murray smiles after him as Rock goes out.

And from Murray's eyes we see Rock walk down the Hallway
towards the main door, which is opened for him by the Porter,
Tom.

II

DINING-ROOM OF ROCK'S HOUSE.

On the large, shining table of the large and handsome room the
candles are lit in their heavy silver candlesticks.

The curtains are drawn.

The furniture of the room is good and solid. There is little orna-
mentation.

At the table sits a woman, writing. There are coffee-things near her.

We *TRACK TOWARDS* her, from the door.

And, close, we see that she is a woman of about forty, with black
hair combed sternly back, strong features, straight unrelenting
mouth: a woman of determination, who knows her own mind
and, though she may not like it, will always speak it.

She is writing, with severe, upright pen strokes, on large white cards.

There is the sound of a door opening.

She looks up from her writing, and says:

ANNABELLA. Oh, Thomas. Can you spare me a moment?

And now, from a little way behind her, we look at Rock standing in
the doorway, hesitant, top-hat in hand.

ROCK. A hundred, my dear Annabella. All my time is
at your disposal, except when I am working or eating or
drinking or sleeping. And so on.

ANNABELLA. Then come in and close the door.

ROCK. I *was* going upstairs to work. I had thought of
completing my Observations on the Structure of the Stomach
of the Peruvian Llama to-night.

ANNABELLA. I doubt if such a creature exists. I think you
invented it as an excuse. And besides, if it does exist, it
probably has no stomach.

Reluctantly Rock comes in and closes the door behind him. He approaches the table.

> ANNABELLA. I want you to look at the invitations, that is all. I may have forgotten someone.
> ROCK. Oh, fortunate someone!

Annabella hands the little pile of cards to Rock. He looks through them, idly.

> ANNABELLA. There is no need to be contemptuous of a celebration in your own honour. It may well be the last if you continue to go around the City capriciously insulting every one, and writing absurd letters to the papers about every subject from salmon-fishing to astronomy, and preaching perverted nonsense to a lot of credulous youths and calling it the new philosophy.
> ROCK. I smell vinegar in the air to-night.

But now he is looking through the cards again, and this time not idly. He speaks in a changed voice.

> ROCK. Why are not Doctor and Mrs. Gregory invited?
> ANNABELLA. Mrs. Gregory will not sit at table with *her*.

She makes a little gesture of her head towards the door. Rock gives no sign of having heard or understood.

> ROCK. And the Nicolsons?
> ANNABELLA. No self-respecting body would sit down at dinner in the presence of . . .
> ROCK. [Interrupting, quickly, but in an expressionless voice.] . . . my wife.
> ANNABELLA. You can't think that you can outrage every convention and not suffer for it. You married her for better or for worse; and it 's worse. I have never understood why you didn't keep the girl as your mistress in some other part of the town.
>
> But no, you have to bring your shabby amours back into the house and *legalize* them.
>
> People have long memories. They don't forget that you

disgraced your name, *and* mine, and defied every social decency when you married . . .

But Rock, silent, is walking to the door, opening it, and going out. He pays no attention to Annabella. She is left standing at the table, her sentence unfinished.

12

STAIRWAY OF ROCK'S HOUSE.

Rock is climbing the stairs. As he climbs we hear the voice of his mind.

> ROCK'S VOICE. . . . When I married Elizabeth. When I said, cool as ice, one morning—cool as fire!—'Elizabeth and I are married.' Oh, the shame and horror on the faces of all the puritanical hyenas, prudery ready to pounce and bite, snobbery braying in all the drawing-rooms and breeding-boxes, false pride and prejudice coming out of their holes, hissing and spitting because a man married for love and not for property or position or for any of the dirty devices of the world . . .

We see him, from below, climbing up, disappearing round one winding corner, then appearing again out of shadow. And the voice of his mind grows softer and, slowly, fades.

13

ELIZABETH'S ROOM.

Elizabeth is sitting near the fire, nursing a young child, as Rock comes in. She looks up. She sees the controlled fury on his face.

> ELIZABETH. Thomas. You have been losing your temper again.

He crosses to her, and looks down at her and the child.

Rock. Not this time. No, my dear, society has been losing its temper with *me*. And you.

Elizabeth. Society. That's a lot of people.

Rock. Oh, Annabella is the priestess of the whole genteel rabble. She speaks for all the slanderers and backbiters from here to hell.

Elizabeth. [Gentle, as throughout.] Was it you and me again?

Rock. Again.

Elizabeth. It makes people so angry, still. They think that if they don't *show* they're angry *all* the doctors and lawyers will be marrying market girls and housemaids . . .

Rock. It would do them good. I wish all the mummified lawyers would marry women of the streets and breed howling families of thieves and vagabonds. I wish the professors would marry their cooks and breed *proper* children, not more little scholars in diapers.

Elizabeth. Oh no, that wouldn't work at all. You are famous. People want to look up to you. They can't do that if you insult them by marrying below you.

Rock. Below me! Love is not below me! What am I? An insensible pedagogue, cold-blooded as a herring, with my nose permanently buried in a body? A mincing old maid of a man with . . .

Elizabeth. No, dear. Which of your friends have been refusing to meet me now? I've only met a few of them. I thought they were very nice and they got up when I came in and called me ma'am . . .

Rock. I do not need any friends. I prefer enemies. They are better company and their feelings towards you are always genuine. No, it is only that some overweening and underbred women, the wives and tormentors of unlucky doctors, have contrived to tell Annabella that they would not accept our invitation to dinner.

Elizabeth. Oh, but they *must*. It's very important. You must be at your best. I want them to respect you. You must tell your sister to send off all the invitations, and at the foot of the ones to the ladies who won't accept because of me you must tell her to write, very nicely, that I won't be able to be present at dinner because I am indisposed.

ROCK. I shall cancel the dinner.

ELIZABETH. You'll do nothing of the sort, Thomas.

ROCK. Then I shall write to tell them that their inability to accept our invitation is obviously due to the fact that they suffer from swine fever, and that I appreciate their delicacy in not wishing to spread it.

ELIZABETH. You'll tell Annabella exactly what I've told you. And now that subject is all over. You haven't asked anything about your son. He couldn't go to sleep to night. He cried and cried. He was frightened. I've had to nurse him to sleep.

Rock kisses Elizabeth. He touches on the forehead the child in her arms.

ROCK. Good night, little boy.

And we *TRACK PAST* Rock towards the window, out of the window and into darkness.

14

Music.

Night.

A graveyard.

Three muffled figures skulk down the graveyard path. One carries a lantern. By the lantern light we see the shapes of the grave stones on either side; some of the graves are thickly spiked and railinged round. And by this light we make out the appearances of the silent, shadowy figures.

One is very tall and thin; he wears a top hat. One, also top hatted, carries some heavy implements; the lantern, for a moment, flickers

17

his way, and we see the shape of a spade, the coils of a heavy chain. The lantern-carrier is a very short man.

Now the lantern-carrier stops at a new grave, and lowers his light. The grave is only a tidy heap of newly turned earth; no stone stands at its head.

We hear the whisper of the lantern-carrier:

> Here it is. This is the one.

The spade-bearer puts down his implements. We hear his whisper:

> Hallelujah.

And the tall, top-hatted man whispers:

> Go to it, Mole.

The short man begins to dig at the end of the grave earth.

And the tall one, looking carefully, slyly, around, whispers again:

> Quiet as death to-night.

And the one who carried the spade whispers in return:

> Praise be the Lord.

The short man digs on. Then, putting down the spade, he whispers:

> The chain!

The tall man hands it to him. We see that the chain has a large hook at the end. We see it thrust into the hole the spade has dug. And we hear the noise of steel knocking on wood.

The chain, in the hands of the short man, wriggles above the earth like a snake.

Steel grates against steel.

The short man whispers:

> It's a hard clasp they've put on the coffin.

His companion whispers:

> . . . The unbelievers.

And the tall man whispers:

> Break it with the spade, then. Hurry. The cold's got into my bones.

The short man pushes his spade through the earth. Spade against steel. The ripping of wood.

18

The tall man whispers:
> Careful.

And the chain is lowered again.

And slowly, out of the earth, comes the head of a man, and then the shrouded shoulders, hauled up by the hook of the chain.

The tall man whispers:
> Easy, easy.   Don't wake him.

Slowly the three men raise up the fourth.

The arm of the dead man drops, stiff, against the lantern.

The lantern goes out.

And suddenly, to loud gay music, we *DISSOLVE* to:

15

INTERIOR OF TAVERN A.

On a bench in a corner sit three men.   No one sits quite next to them, though the tavern is crowded.   We recognize them as the three men of the graveyard.   All three are drunk, though solemnly as befits men whose business is death.

The very tall top-hatted man (Andrew Merry-Lees) is a cadaverous clown; a deacon of the drinking-cellar, a pillar of unrespectability.

The other top-hatted man (Praying Howard) has an almost benevolent, almost sweet and saintly, appearance run to seed and whisky.

The short man (Mole) is very hairy; almost furry, like a mole.

They raise their tankards to each other.

> ANDREW MERRY-LEES. To the dead!
>
> PRAYING HOWARD. To the Surgeons of our City!

They drink.

Now we see, sitting quite close to them, the two men of the Market-place.   They are listening hard, but cautiously, to the other three.

> MOLE. It's been a good month.   I'm thirsty.
>
> PRAYING HOWARD. A blessed month.
>
> ANDREW MERRY-LEES. Subjects like penny pies.   Plenty

of 'em. I'm thirsty too, Mole. I've drunk three pints o'
gin. And I'm goin' to drink *three pints more* . . .

PRAYING HOWARD. Careful, careful, Andrew, you 'll get the
taste for it.

And the three of them croak and laugh, without smiling, like three
carrion-crows.

And the two men of the Market are listening all the time.

The short, squat man beckons, secretly, with a stubby black finger,
to an old woman, all rags and bones, standing drinking near them.

Coming closer, we hear his whisper:

Who would they be with all that money for the drink?

The woman looks, with frightened eyes, at the croakers in the
corner. Then she whispers:

Andrew Merry-Lees, and Praying Howard, and . . . [her
voice goes softer] . . . the Mole.

And the squat man questions her again, in a rough, Irish whisper:

And what do they do for a living, my lovey?

She answers, in a sharp whisper full of fear:

Body-snatchers.

He makes a movement as though to cross himself, then lets his hand
fall, and looks at his companion.

We see the thin side-twisted lips of his companion frame the syllables:

Body-snatchers.

They look at each other as the camera *TRACKS BACK* to show
the whole tavern and the three solemnly croaking, laughing men
in the corner.

DISSOLVE TO

16

DINING-ROOM OF ROCK'S HOUSE.
There are eight gentlemen at table.
The port is being passed.

Through the general conversation we hear:

GREEN. I was sorry to hear that Mrs. Rock was indisposed, Thomas. Only once I had the honour ...

FIRST GENTLEMAN. Nothing, I hope? ...

ROCK. [Shaking his head.] ... Serious. ... The child. ... The weather ...

SECOND GENTLEMAN. [Nodding in the direction of Murray across the table.] I was asking Mr. Murray, purely out of academic interest, why body-snatchers are known as Resurrectionists. He was polite enough to excuse my morbidity so soon after dinner, but ...

MURRAY. I'm afraid I was rather uncertain myself. Thomas can tell you.

GREEN. Thomas knows *every* answer. I sometimes suspect him of prearranging the questions so that his encyclopaedic information can come rolling 'spontaneously' out.

ROCK. You overestimate me, Doctor Green. I can answer every question only *after dinner* when people are usually not in a position to verify my facts. But Mr. Sinclair's question is too simple. The removal of a body from the walled precincts of God's Acre was viewed by the superstitious and the credulous as nothing less than an interference with the plans of Providence and the Great Resurrection. So the poor ghoul of a body-snatcher became a 'Resurrectionist.'

THIRD GENTLEMAN. If by the superstitious and the credulous you mean believers in Christianity, Doctor Rock ...

ROCK. Sir, I did not say a superstitious and credulous Christian any more than Brahmin or Buddhist or Worshipper of Elephants. If I say, in conversation, that I know a woman who is opinionated, vicious, and ugly, I *do* distrust the man who immediately says: 'Sir, you are talking about my mother!'

THIRD GENTLEMAN. If Logic itself came to dine with you, you would give it an excellent dinner and then try to strangle it. All I wanted to say was that as a Christian I deplore the sacrilege of digging up the dead for anatomists to dissect.

FIRST GENTLEMAN. [To no one in particular.] I wish I had retired with the ladies.

ROCK. I am no platform drummer, no hawker of slogans, but I say that the Resurrectionists who dig up the dead and sell them to the Anatomical Schools are a direct result of the wrongness of the Law. The Law says that surgeons must possess a high degree of skill. And a surgeon cannot acquire that skill without working upon dead human beings. But the Law also says that the only dead human beings we *can* work upon must come from the public gallows; a very uncertain, and meagre, supply. Legally, the hangman is our one provider. But he would have to hang all the *liars* in the City or all the men who are unfaithful to their wives, before there would be sufficient subjects for us. Therefore, we have to obtain our bodies illegally.

I myself, last term, had to pay out five hundred guineas to the Resurrectionists.

Rock drinks.

Murray passes the port to the Second Gentleman. The Second Gentleman fills his glass.

SECOND GENTLEMAN. [Aside.] What very good port they provide in a mortuary these days . . .

But Rock now has the attention of the whole table.

ROCK. Do not suppose for a moment that, even after dinner and in one of those mellow, argumentative moods in which one would try to prove that black is white or that politicians are incorruptible, I regard the Resurrectionists as anything but the vicious human vermin of the gutters of the city; in fact, a pack of devils.

But as the Law says 'No' to our need, to the need of progressive science, so up crawl these creatures to satisfy that

22

need *against* the Law. The same applies to every city, though *ours* is rather more fortunate than most; it is *full* of perverted blackguards.

GREEN. [Provokingly.] If you dislike so much the Law that applies to your own science, Thomas, why did you become an anatomist rather than anything else?

ROCK. There was more body to it.

FIRST GENTLEMAN. You would make our City sound to a stranger like Sodom or Gomorrah. . . .

GREEN. It *is* a seat of learning, after all, Thomas . . .

ROCK. And the bowels of squalor. Look any night at the streets of this 'cultured city.' Observe, with academic calm, the homeless and the hopeless and the insane and the wretchedly drunken lying in their rags on the stinking cobbles. Look for yourselves, sirs, at the beggars, and the cripples, and the tainted children, and the pitiful, doomed girls. Write a scholastic pamphlet on the things that prowl in the alleys, afraid to see the light; they were men and women once. Be proud of *that* if you can.

In the silence that follows, Murray rises to his feet.

MURRAY. If you'll excuse me, gentlemen, I must try to brave this—'*terrible* city at night.' You'll excuse me?

At a smiling nod—for Rock has again, suddenly, changed mood— Murray bows and goes out of the room.

ROCK. [At his most jocularly donnish.] And now, gentle-men, no more such talk from me.

SECOND GENTLEMAN. Oh, surely, not a little entertaining gossip about cannibalism, for a change?

ROCK. No, no, no, not another word. Or, as my friend Murray would say, 'Let us change the subject.'

LONG SHOT of the dinner table, Rock at the head, waggishly professional.

17

CITY STREET.

Music.

Night.

Murray is walking along the middle of the street. On both sides
of the street are many ragged bodies, of men, women, and children.
Some are stretched out asleep; some are sprawled drunk, their
hands still clutching a bottle; some are huddled together, like
large, dishevelled birds, for company and warmth. A few have
not managed to reach the comparative shelter of the sides of the
street, but lie, ungainly outcasts, snoring scarecrows and men of
garbage, across the cobbled middle. Over these bodies Murray
steps quickly, carelessly.

CUT to

18

Another humanity-littered CITY STREET, with Murray walking
along it.

CUT to

19

DOORWAY OF ROCK'S ACADEMY.

Murray is knocking at the door.
The door opens slowly, only a few inches at first, then we hear a
husky voice from within.

> VOICE. Och, it's you, Mr. Murray.
> MURRAY. Open up, Tom.

And the door is quickly opened wide. Murray goes in.

24

20

HALLWAY OF ROCK'S ACADEMY.

Murray stands waiting in the gloom of the Hallway while Tom closes
the door.

Tom has a candle in his hand. He moves hurriedly in front of
Murray and leads the way through the darkness down the Hall.

> TOM. I thought it might be another *subject*, sir, at this time of
> night. There was one brought in only an hour ago . . .
> [In a whisper.] By you know who. Andrew and . . .
> MURRAY. Shut your mouth.

They reach a door at the end of the Hall.

Murray opens the door. Tom, with his candle, scuttles back into
the darkness.

21

DISSECTING ROOM OF ROCK'S ACADEMY.

Night.

A large room, cold, clean, and echoing.

Tables and slabs.

Anatomical diagrams on the walls.

On one of the tables we see an array of shining instruments: knives,
saws, choppers, and long sharp steel tools.

The room is lit by one flickering gas-jet.

Two young men stand at one of the tables.

On it we see, half in shadow, a shrouded body wrapped in sacking.

Murray is coming into the room.

> MURRAY. [Brusquely.] Evening, Brown . . . 'ning, Harding.

Murray crosses to the table. He unwraps the sacking, flings aside
a few soiled white cloths, lowers his hand in between them.

For a moment there is silence.

> MURRAY. Stand out of the light, will you?

Suddenly he flings back the cloths, and straightens up.

MURRAY. [In angry undertone.] Ugh! This is a week old! Why can't the fools bring something fresh? Don't they get paid enough? Might as well dissect a dog dragged out of the river after the fishes have been at it. Come on, let's go and have a drink in the market. *That*'s not worth pickling. Come on.

He walks towards the door, opens it, stands waiting.
Harding lowers the gas.
And out of the dim room the three of them walk into darkness.
And out of the darkness comes loud, gay music, and we are in:

22

INTERIOR OF TAVERN B.

Shouts and laughter, and a wet dribble of singing.
The benches are packed tight with beggars, hawkers, cheap-jacks, drunks, street women, rogues, and slummers.
The rough tables are crowded with tankards and bottles, stained with spilt drink.
At the open doorway, children rabble together.
Moving slowly down the room, we pass the two women whom last we saw crying 'Rags and bones' and 'Cat-skin' through the Market.
In their bedraggled shawls and cock-eyed bonnets they look as though they might have been made out of their own wares.
Moving slowly down, we pass, near the two women, a beautiful girl of about twenty years who has spent nearly half of them trying to defeat her beauty. She is giggling, half tipsy, at some unpleasantry.
Moving slowly down we pass Andrew Merry-Lees and Praying Howard. Sober as churchyard worms, in their corpse-dusty top-hats, they are trying to cure the hiccups of Mole—who sits, small and furry, between them—by pouring drink from a tankard down his throat.
Moving slowly down, we reach Murray and the two young students,

Brown and Harding, with tankards before them. They are, all three, a little tight and talkative.

> BROWN. Refined gathering to-night.
> HARDING. Too refined for old Murray after his hurly-burly with the great. How did the dinner go?
> MURRAY. Thomas was on top of the world.
> BROWN. Gracious, loquacious, insulting, exulting . . .
> HARDING. [Overtopping him.] . . . drastic, bombastic, charming, disarming . . .
> BROWN. [Not to be outdone, with extravagant gestures.] . . . avuncular, carbuncular.
> HARDING. What did he talk about at dinner, apart from sex and religion and politics?
> MURRAY. Body-snatchers.

Harding, with a 'Sh!' of warning, gives Murray a dig with his elbow, and nods up the room to where Merry-Lees and the Mole are now solemnly pouring whisky down Praying Howard.

As Murray looks in their direction, so he sees the beautiful girl and beckons her over to him.

Beautifully unsteady, she approaches. Brown and Harding squeeze up to make room for her beside Murray.

> MURRAY. Sit down and drink with us, sweet Jennie Bailey, my lovely charmer. . . .

CUT to the two Market women looking with undisguised dislike at Jennie Bailey, Murray, and the two students, who are now drinking and laughing together.

The first of the women, she who cried the cry of 'Rags and bones,' is soddenly morose, a coarse slattern and drab.

The second woman, she who cried the cry of 'Cat-skin,' is a bawd and virago.

The first woman says:

> Look at Jennie Bailey, the lady. Drinking with the doctors. Look at her, Kate.

KATE. I'd like to be putting my nails in her eyes. . . . I saw that Bob Fallon looking at her yesterday. Mind your step, Nelly.

NELLY. She won't be young for long. Another year and the men won't look at her. She's the sort that grows old in a night.

I seen your Mr. Broom looking at her, too. Showing all his teeth.

KATE. She wouldn't go with Fallon or Broom, not she. Look at her. Not when there's money.

CUT to *CLOSE SHOT* of Murray and Jennie. They are sitting close together. Brown and Harding have moved away from them, further down the table.

MURRAY. Why can't we meet in another place, sometimes, Jennie? Anywhere else, not always in this damned tavern, with all the sluts and drunks staring at us.

JENNIE. Where else *could* you take me, sweetheart, except for a walk in the fields—and in winter too! Kissing in a hedge in the snow like two robins.

MURRAY. We could find somewhere to be together.

JENNIE. Loving in the lanes, with all the trees dripping down your back and the thorns tearing your petticoats, and little insects wriggling all over you—oh no! Or sitting holding hands in your lodgings all the evening, and your brother studying books in the other corner! [Softly.] You know you could come home with me.

MURRAY. And you know that I won't. I *can't*! Don't you understand that I couldn't go back with you there. Not there, in that house. I don't want to think of you in that house, ever. I don't want to think of the others, and your smiling at them and letting them . . .

JENNIE. Oh, the 'others' don't mean a thing in the wide world. They're *different*. I'm for *you*. Come back; now. I'll tell Rosie you're staying and . . .

MURRAY. No. No, Jennie. Please. You're *beautiful*. Come

28

away. Come away from everything here. Are you never
going to say 'Yes' to me, even if I ask you a thousand
thousand times! I 'm asking you again, Jennie . . .

JENNIE. [Gaily.] Oh, a fine young doctor's wife I'd make.
Wouldn't the ladies love me? 'And from what part do
you come, Mrs. Murray?' 'Number 23 Pigs' Yard.
Your husband used to call on Wednesdays.' . . .

CUT to the door of the tavern, where the two men of the Grass-
market, the tall, thin, always half-dancing one, and the squat one,
are standing.

They look round the room.

They see Kate and Nelly, and make their way across the crowded,
swirling bar towards them.

The tall one crackles his way through the crowd, jumping and
finger-snapping, a long damp leer stuck on the side of his face.

The squat one elbows his way through, now sullenly truculent, now
oily and almost bowing.

They stand over their women.

And the squat man says, ingratiatingly and yet with an under-
menace:

> Can you buy a little drink for us, Nelly darling? We 're
> thirsty, love.

And the thin man says, in his high, mad voice:

> Can you buy a little drink for Fallon and Broom, Fallon
> and Broom. . . .

He makes the grotesque movements of drinking, still finger-snapping,
one shoulder higher than the other.

> NELLY. There 's money for two more and that 's all. Here,
> buy 'em yourself, Bob Fallon.

She tosses Fallon a coin. And as he catches the coin and shoulders
the few steps to the bar, Broom reaches for Nelly's drink. Nelly
makes as if to snatch the tankard back, but Broom suddenly shows
his teeth and pretends to snap at her.

KATE. Ach, leave him be. Broom s got the devil in him to-night. He'd bite your hand through. I know him.

By this time Fallon has returned with two drinks, and hands one to Broom, who attacks it hungrily again.

Fallon, from under his heavy, hanging eyebrows, stares around the bar. Suddenly he sees Merry-Lees and the two others.

FALLON. [To the women.] There's the three . . . [His voice lowers.] . . . snatchers we see in the 'Old Bull.' They're swillin' the drink again. Must've digged up another to-night.

He turns to look at Broom, who is staring at the three Resurrectionists with glinting, unseeing eyes.

FALLON. Fourteen pounds for a corpse they get when it's digged up new. . . . Fourteen pounds! . . .

BROOM. [In his high, loud voice.] Fourteen pounds for gin and pies . . .

KATE. Hush! you mad dog. . . .

NELLY. There's no more left.

She gets up and goes towards the door. Fallon follows her, Broom and Kate behind him. As they move through the bar to the door, we hear Fallon whine:

FALLON. Come on, Nelly darlin', scrape up a penny or two for a drop for us . . . There's plenty of ways, lovey . . .

23

THE MARKET-PLACE, OUTSIDE TAVERN B.

Moonlight.

The noise of the tavern swirls in a hiccuping gust out into the street.

The Market stalls are shrouded like dead-carts.

And the doors of other pubs and houses are open, staining light out on to the cobbles.

People stand at doorways, up to no good.

People and other pigs flop on the strawed cobbles.

Nelly walks to a barrow just outside the pub and takes the handles. The barrow is heaped with rags.

Fallon, Broom, and Kate follow her as she begins to push the barrow through the moonlit Market.

Suddenly, with a yelp, Broom leaps on to the barrow, sitting bolt upright among the rags.

> BROOM. [In a high, gay snarl.]
>> Broom
>> In his carriage and pair . . .

Nelly takes no notice but doggedly pushes the barrow on.

And sullenly Fallon walks at the side, Kate trailing after him.

> FALLON. Fourteen pounds for a corpse! . . .

They move out of the Market, through the alleyways.

> NELLY. [In a harsh grumble as she trundles the barrow on with its load of rags and one cackling man.] Why don't you dig one up yourself? You 're frightened of the dark..

Over the cobbles of lonely alleys the barrow rattles, and the finger-snapping, dog-haired man squatting on the rags points his finger at one dark doorway, then at another.

> BROOM. They 're dead in there. . . . Dig 'em up, Fallon.
> . . . In there. . . . In there. . . .

Round a corner they come into Rag-and-Bone Alley.

24

RAG-AND-BONE ALLEY.

They stop at the door of a tenement.

In a first-floor window hangs a sign:

> CLEAN BEDS

Kate opens the door and goes through. Fallon follows her. Broom leaps from the barrow and is inside the dark doorway like a weasel into a hole.

LARGE LODGING-ROOM.

The four of them are moving through the room.

Around the walls of the room are many narrow beds.

Some of these beds are occupied. By men, or by women, or by human beings at all, we cannot see, but we can hear the noises of unhappy sleep, the sodden snore, the broken sigh, the whimpering of breath.

The four move through the room towards a small open door.

The two women go through the door into the darkness of the adjoining room.

Fallon stops at the last two beds against the wall. He looks down upon them.

In each of them sleeps an old man covered with rags.

One old man is mumbling in his sleep the almost inaudible scraps and ends of prayer.

And as Fallon looks down upon him, Broom tiptoes to his side.

Silently Fallon and Broom look down upon the two old sleeping men, whose hideously haggard faces for a moment we see close.

26

LECTURE HALL OF ROCK'S ACADEMY.

CLOSE-UP of Rock lecturing. He has a large volume in his hand.

> ROCK. This, gentlemen, is a volume by Vesalius, the acknowledged father of our art. Look at its size, and bear in mind that its thousand folio pages . . .

From Rock's angle we look down at the densely packed auditorium of his Lecture Hall. Among the faces of the students we recognize those of Brown and Harding.

> ROCK. [Continuing throughout.] . . . embrace only a special part of the human anatomy. . . . Now, gentlemen . . .

From the auditorium we look up at Rock as, with a very small
   volume in his other hand, he continues:

> ROCK. . . . . behold the advance of the age, the progress of
> science to-day, the *Pocket Anatomist,* said to contain the
> *whole* of Anatomy within the compass of three inches by two.

Reverently he lays down the large volume on his lecturing table.
With the greatest contempt he casts the small volume across the
   platform.
Laughter of the students.

27

PRIVATE SMOKEROOM IN AN INN.

A snug little box of a room that could not hold more than four.
Two small oak settles facing each other.
A fire-place. A blazing wood fire.
A mantelpiece. A shining ebony clock. On either side of the
   clock, a tall silver candlestick. Candles burning.
A little counter. Behind the counter, bottles gleaming in candle-
   light.
Two old gentlemen are seated in the room. They have an air of
   judicious, contented permanency. They seem part of the furni-
   ture; their baldness gleams like the silver, like the mellow bottles.
   Each holds a silver tankard.

> FIRST GENTLEMAN. Now if I had a boy . . .
> SECOND GENTLEMAN. . . . . He'd be no boy now, John . . .
> FIRST GENTLEMAN. . . . . If I had a boy and he decided to
>   enter the medical profession—against my wishes, needless to
>   say; the legal profession has always been good enough for
>   us—I would no more send him to Thomas Rock than I'd
>   lay down the law to my wife. Your health!
> SECOND GENTLEMAN. Health!
> FIRST GENTLEMAN. They tell me, for example, that he openly
>   condones the activities of the Resurrectionists. . . .

SECOND GENTLEMAN. He married a young person who was in domestic employment, too, I believe. . . .

FIRST GENTLEMAN. No, Richard, my wife tells me that she sold fish. . . .

SECOND GENTLEMAN. It is all the same—fish or dish-clouts.

FIRST GENTLEMAN. And I have heard that he has a most scurrilous tongue. . . . Preaches Anarchy. . . . Ridicules the Law. . . . Has all his young men *laughing*, and spouting revolutionary doctrine. . . . Interpolates violent criticisms of the Constitution in the very middle of his supposedly scientific lectures. . . . He does not even try to live like a gentleman. . . . My wife says that they keep only *one* maid in the whole house. . . .

SECOND GENTLEMAN. Mrs. Rock can do the rest of the work, I suppose. She is used to it.

FIRST GENTLEMAN. No, no, Richard, she sold fish. . . .

SECOND GENTLEMAN. Another, John?

FIRST GENTLEMAN. Thank you. . . . No more than a double. . . .

The First Gentleman raises his hand in a restraining gesture.

DISSOLVE to

28

Bright sunshine.

Students rushing pell-mell across THE SQUARE towards Rock's Academy.

A baker, carrying a big wooden tray of loaves across the Square, only just manages to avoid them.

We see the students race up the sreps.

29

We see the students in the LECTURE HALL OF ROCK'S ACADEMY.
Rock enters.

He enters like a great actor; he acknowledges the ovation of his

34

audience; he bows; he steps to the platform table; he adjusts his spectacles and his cuffs; every movement is studied.

ROCK. Gentlemen . . .

DISSOLVE to

30

LECTURE HALL AT NIGHT.

The hall is dimly lit.

Rock, in shirt-sleeves, is rehearsing a lecture to an audience of one solitary skeleton.

ROCK. . . . And are we to be told that the Kafir is a savage because he lives in the wilds, and that John Bull is the happy creature of civilization because he wears breeches, learns catechism, and cheats his neighbours? I say that . . .

During this rehearsal, the door of the Lecture Hall opens slowly, and two very young students poke their heads around to watch the master in uncomprehension and awe.

31

CLOSE-UP of two elderly professors, in mortar-boards and gowns, standing against the background of a very large, ornately gold-framed portrait of another old professor.

FIRST PROFESSOR. I knew him when he was a boy. He was clever as a monkey, and he looked like one, too. But he was never *really young*.

SECOND PROFESSOR. Or sound.

FIRST PROFESSOR. No, one cannot say one likes him, or approves of him. But that is not the question. We must disregard personal prejudice.

SECOND PROFESSOR. Difficult, when *he* refuses to disregard it. He called me 'insipid booby' in the *Scientific Journal*. . . .

FIRST PROFESSOR. [With a side glance at his companion.] Most uncalled for. No, my point is that one cannot look upon him as an insignificant opponent. His medical history is, unfortunately, brilliant. And they *do* think very highly of him on the Continent. Add to that, that he has five hundred students attending his classes, and that his nearest rival, our old friend Hocking, has less than a dozen. . . .

SECOND PROFESSOR. Nine, to be exact, and that includes three nephews. . . .

FIRST PROFESSOR. . . . and we begin to see what a pernicious influence the fellow might have upon the whole scholastic life of the City; indeed, upon the trend of scholastic thought *everywhere*. . . .

SECOND PROFESSOR. A menace. A menace. So rude, too. . . .

32

ROCK LECTURING.

He holds a human skull high in his hands.

33

CLOSE SHOT, from above, of an Old Man lying in his coffin.

We recognize him as one of the two old men who were sleeping when Fallon and Broom looked down at them in Sequence 25.

The lid of the coffin comes down.

TRACK BACK to show that we are in the Large Lodging-room of Fallon and Broom's house.

A Coffin Carpenter is nailing the coffin which lies at the foot of a bed. The straw of the bed lies scattered round it.

In the next bed, the other Old Man, wrapped in his rags, is staring at

the coffin, at the Carpenter, and at Fallon and Broom, who stand
at the entrance to the small adjoining room.
The rest of the beds in the Lodging-room are empty.

> BROOM. Hammer him in, hammer him in. Four pounds
> rent all dead in a box.
>
> FALLON. Now who would've thought old Daniel could be
> so mean. Dying without a word, and owing us four
> pounds. He didn't even have a penny piece hidden under
> the straw. . . .
>
> BROOM. If only he was alive again so that I could kill him
> with my hands. . . .
>
> FALLON. And all he left was a bit of a broken pipe. . . .
> And livin' here all these months on the fat of the land.
> . . . Many's the night I've beaten the rats off him my-
> self. . . .

Fallon is slouched against the doorway in a kind of self-pitying
gloom, but Broom is half dancing with rage. . . .
The Carpenter goes on hammering.

> BROOM. Four pounds gone! Whisky and gin and bonnets
> gone! No more money for Broom! Hammer him in—
> hammer him in!
>
> COFFIN CARPENTER. [Without looking up.] And what
> do you think I'm doing? Pullin' him out?

The beating of the hammer on the nails of the coffin.
And slowly Broom's dancing fury dies; he swivels his eyes towards
Fallon.
Fallon looks back at him, and slowly through his mulish blood-
shot stupidity he seems to understand.
Now the Carpenter rises, collects his tools, goes out through the
far door.

> FALLON. [In a heavy whisper.] Hammer him in, hammer
> him in . . .
>
> BROOM. [Softly.] . . . and what do you think I'm doing
> . . . [More loudly.] . . . pullin' him out?

Broom runs swiftly to the far door, looks out, turns back, slams the
door, bolts it, runs back. . . .

>   BROOM. Four pounds he owes us and ten pounds they 'll give
>   us for him. . . .
>   FALLON. [With a kind of sodden horror.] Body-snatchers!

But Broom is calling through the other door:

>   BROOM. Kate, Kate, come here!

Nelly and Kate come in.

>   BROOM. Here, take one end.   Take his head.

Without understanding, the women obey, take hold of the top of
the coffin while Broom takes the other.   Together they drag the
coffin through the door into the other room.   Still Fallon does
not move.

Then, suddenly, he draws back his heavy, muscle-bound shoulders,
and follows them.

And the eyes of the Old Man in the bed follow *him*.

We hear whispering from the other room.

Then a scraping, screwing noise.

Then the door is shut.

34

CITY STREET.

Late evening.

We see, in *LONG SHOT*, Fallon and Broom moving up the
street away from camera.

Fallon is carrying a tea-chest on his back.

By his side, at a zany trot, goes Broom.

We see two policemen coming slowly down the street towards them
and towards us.

And Fallon and Broom move quickly and suddenly down a side
street.

ANOTHER CITY STREET.

Late evening.

Fallon and Broom walking along with the tea-chest.

Two students pass them.

Broom nudges Fallon, who puts down the tea-chest and follows them a few steps.

> FALLON. [In his whining voice.] Beg your pardon me askin', sirs, if it's not too much trouble for you, could you be telling me where the Academy is? We've a little matter of business . . .

The students have paused and turned round.

> FIRST STUDENT. What Academy do you want?
> SECOND STUDENT. . . . And what's the little business? Oh!

The Second Student has seen the tea-chest a little way off, with Broom, its attendant, winking and leering.

He draws the First Student's attention to the tea-chest.

> FIRST STUDENT. If it's a subject . . .

Fallon cringes, and nods, and nods again.

> FIRST STUDENT. . . . take it along to Doctor Rock's. That's over there. Round that corner. It's the second house in the square. He'll pay you a better price than Hocking.
> FALLON. Oh yes, that was the name, sirs, Hocking, sirs, Hocking. . . .
> FIRST STUDENT. You take it to Doctor Rock. . . .
> FALLON. Oh, thank you, sirs, thank you, my humblest thanks to you, sirs. . . .

But the two students have walked off.

And Fallon rejoins the tea-chest and Broom, and lifts the tea-chest on his back and moves on. . . .

36

DOORWAY OF ROCK'S ACADEMY.

Broom raps at the door, then quickly steps back, ready to run.

Fallon, with the tea-chest, stands, bowed, near the door, stubbornly servile.

The grille in the door opens, and the face of Tom stares through: a face through a spider-web.

Through the grille, through Tom's eyes, we see the two men: the barrel-bulk of Fallon in the foreground, the lean lank Broom craning a little way behind him.

> FALLON. [Ingratiatingly.] Two young gentlemen told us we could sell an article here. . . . We got it in the tea-chest. . . .

Now, from Fallon's eyes, we see the face of Tom at the grille.

> TOM. [With a grunt.] Wait.

The grille closes. Bolts rattle. The door opens slowly.

We hear Tom's voice from the darkness within the door, but we do not see him.

> TOM'S VOICE. Come in. Walk quiet.

From behind them we see Fallon and Broom walk into the darkness. The door closes.

37

HALLWAY OF ROCK'S ACADEMY.

In the gloom, what stands within the tall, glass-fronted cases that line the Hallway cannot clearly be seen. But Fallon and Broom glance quickly, fearfully, at them, and we catch for a moment the glint of a bone, the shape of a stripped head.

Tom beckons, and walks down the Hall towards the door under the stairs.

> TOM. Follow. Walk quiet.

Fallon and Broom follow him into the small, dark, bare Cloak-room.

> TOM. Put it down there. Wait. Don't move now.

Tom goes out, leaving Fallon and Broom standing one at each side of the tea-chest in the dark room.

Tom walks into the Hall, climbs the stairs.

38

CORRIDOR IN ROCK'S ACADEMY.

Tom walks along the Corridor. He stops at a door.

From within we hear the voice of Rock:

> ROCK'S VOICE. . . . It was Herophilus who first traced the arachnoid membrane into the ventricles of the brain and . . .

Tom knocks three times on the door, and we hear Rock interrupt his sentence to say:

> ROCK'S VOICE. Come in.

And Tom enters.

From the open door we see into:

39

REFERENCE LIBRARY IN ROCK'S ACADEMY.

It is a smallish book-lined room, in which Rock is talking, informally, to a small group of seated students. He is walking up and down before them, his arms behind his back, but he stops at sight of Tom and raises his eyebrows questioningly.

> TOM. [In a confidential voice.] There's a couple of new hands downstairs, sir, they've brought . . .

But Rock, turning to the students, interrupts him.

> ROCK. Excuse me, gentlemen, you and Herophilus must wait a few moments.

And he walks out of the room, Tom stepping back to allow him
   passage.
Then Tom follows him.

40

CORRIDOR IN ROCK'S ACADEMY.

We follow Rock and Tom along the Corridor, down the stairs, and
   into the Hallway.
They go into the Cloak-room under the stairs.

41

SMALL CLOAK-ROOM.

Fallon and Broom move aside nervously into the shadows as Rock,
   taking no notice of them at all, goes straight to the tea-chest.
Tom hurries to his side, cuts the ropes around the chest, drags away
   the straw and rags.
Rock looks inside.
Then he straightens up, takes out a purse, hands it to Tom.

   ROCK. Give them seven pounds ten.

As Tom opens the purse and counts out the money from it, Rock,
   for the first time, looks at Fallon and Broom.

   ROCK. What are your names?

Fallon steps, toadying, out of the shadows.

   FALLON. Bob Fallon, sir.

Rock nods towards the shadows.

   ROCK. And the other?

Broom comes out, like a ghost, smiling his long side smile, but he
   does not speak. His long fingers rap-rap-rap on his elbow.

   FALLON. Broom, sir.
   ROCK. If you have any more, let us have them.

Rock turns away and walks out of the room. And Tom hands
   over the money to Fallon.

CITY SQUARE.

Music.

Fallon and Broom are moving through the moonlit Square towards us, Rock's Academy behind them.

Broom is half dancing, finger-snapping, his whole body one long lean grin.

Fallon, at his side clinking coins in his hand, is shambling an accompanying dance.

Nearer, nearer, they dance towards us until their faces fill the screen; until all we can see is the thick snout-mouth and the thin fox-lips, the little glinting eyes and the slant slits.

43

INTERIOR OF TAVERN B.

Closely we see, at a table, the faces of Fallon, Broom, Nelly, and Kate.

Coming closer, at the level of the table, we move past mugs and bottle to a pile of coins and Fallon's hands around them. The hands move, pushing some of the coins across the table.

> FALLON'S VOICE. For you, Nelly love. All for yourself. For you, Kate.

Now, still closely, we see the four at the table.

> FALLON. Broom and I share the rest.

And Fallon divides, in one movement of his broad fingers like big toes, the remaining coins.
Broom snatches his coins up.

> BROOM. A bottle, a bottle, another bottle!

And he darts away from the table and brings a bottle back and pours whisky into each mug.

NELLY. [Softly, in a kind of drunken, lumpish amazement.] Seven pounds ten for an *old* man. . . .

And they all drink.

FALLON. Oh, the shame that he wasn't a *young* man. . . .

And, with their own kinds of laughter, they drink again.

44

MARKET-PLACE.

Day.

Fallon and Broom are looking at the wares on a clothes-stall.

They plough and scatter through the clothes, while the stall-keeper, a fat woman smoking a pipe, looks on expressionlessly.

Fallon pulls out a shawl from a heap of oddments and tosses a coin to the woman who, still expressionlessly but with the deftness of a trained seal, catches it.

FALLON. I 'll have this . . .

He pulls out another shawl, and a skirt, and a petticoat.

FALLON. . . . and this . . . and this . . . and this . . .

And Broom has decked himself with lace from the stall and is mincing around in the parody of a drunken woman.

Fallon, with a wide, extravagant gesture, piles all his presents under his arm, and tosses the woman another coin. She catches it.

And Broom still prances, now with a bonnet on his head.

BROOM. Look at me. . . . look at me. My *mother* wouldn't know me. . . .

And Fallon and Broom link arms and move away through the Market, Broom in his fineries, Fallon trailing a shawl behind him in the mud of the cobbles.

Arm in arm they move on through the Market, to the distant playing of a fiddle.

45

CITY PARK.

Music.

A windy afternoon.

Rock and Elizabeth are walking down a path under the trees.
Annabella walks a little way apart from them, stiffly, primly.

Some way in front of them two little children are running along and
playing.

Through the music we hear the voice of Rock's mind.

> ROCK'S VOICE. Oh, such a cold day for walking abroad,
> and the wind like a drunk beggar with his fiddle. Well,
> I suppose it does us good. It does *me* good to feel the family
> man again, walking through the respectable, gusty park
> with Elizabeth on my arm. . . . Oh, the years fly! Time
> with his wingèd chariot, hurrying near, and my life going
> true and even, and my children growing, and Elizabeth
> with me for ever, and books to write, and work to do. . . .
> Lord, but it's a happy time . . . even in the unhappy
> times. . . .

Slowly, sedately, they move on through the cold afternoon.

46

RAG-AND-BONE ALLEY.

Slowly, disconsolately, Fallon and Broom walk down the Alley
towards the Lodging-house.

Broom is no longer dancing, finger-snapping, pirouetting, but walks
like a wraith, holding his shabby thinness against the cold; and
Fallon, head down, shambles without seeing or caring.

They reach the Lodging-house.

47

All the beds are empty, the earth-coloured blankets flung half off them.

All the beds except one: that bed nearest to the door of the small adjoining room, in which the second Old Man lies still under his filth and rags.

Fallon and Broom walk past the Old Man, open the door of the small room.

His eyes follow them.

The door closes.

48

SMALL ROOM IN LODGING-HOUSE.

In one corner a straw bed.

In another, heaps of rags.

There is a table, a few broken chairs.

Straw and broken glass litter the foul floor.

Fallon throws himself on to the straw bed.

Broom walks about the room, caged, his eyes darting sharply at every squalor.

> FALLON. And what d' you think you'll find? Prowling like a cat. D' you think there's money in the old straw?

Broom has stopped at the cobwebbed window and is looking out.

> BROOM. There's fat pigs in the yard outside.
>
> FALLON. [Not listening.] Drain the dry bottles, lick the floor, scrabble in the muck for a farthing. There's nothing, nothing.
>
> BROOM. [Still at the window.] Fat, juicy porkers waiting for the knife to cut them ear to ear. Squeeeel!
>
> FALLON. Shut your squeal. Ach, if old Daniel was here, dying again!
>
> BROOM. [In a quiet voice, still looking out of the window.] Geordie's dying.

Without turning from the window, Broom nods back at the door
between the small room and the large room.

We move towards Broom.

> BROOM. Geordie coughs all night. Krawf! Krawf!

We move closer to Broom.

> BROOM. [Softly, but clearly.] It's awful *tedious* waiting for
> Geordie to die. . . .

We are right up to Broom's face.

There is complete silence.

Then there is the sound of the rustle of straw. Then the sound of
a door opening

Still Broom does not look round.

Only when a cry comes from the next room, a cry like an old sheep's,
half moan and half bleat, does Broom spin round like a dancer at a cue.

We see him, in CLOSE-UP, staring towards the other room.
Staring. And smiling.

DISSOLVE.

49

CITY STREET.

Music.

Late evening.

LONG SHOT of Fallon and Broom walking away from camera.

Fallon carries the tea-chest on his back.

Broom capers at his side.

50

LARGE LODGING-ROOM.

Kate and Nelly walking through the room.

They stop at the Old Man's bed.

Nelly leans down to look at the empty bed. Then she straightens
up with a little shudder.

And Kate looks.

Silently they pull up the rags and bits of blanket from where they
  have been pulled on to the floor, and cover the straw bed with
  them, carefully, like two housewives.

Suddenly, from outside, there is a loud knocking on the door.

The women start, look at each other.

> NELLY. [Whispering.] Perhaps that's the . . .
> KATE. [Whispering.] Perhaps it's . . . lodgers.

And straightening her dirty shawls about her, she walks down the
  room to see.

51

HALLWAY OF ROCK'S ACADEMY.

Tom is climbing the stairs. From the foot of the stairs we see him
  climb.

He is half-way up when Rock, with top-hat and stick, comes down.

Tom stops.

As Rock approaches him, Tom speaks:

> TOM. It's Bob Fallon and Broom again, sir. They've
>   brought a new subject. It's an old man. He's not . . .
>   very long dead. They want ten pounds, sir.
> ROCK. Give it to them.

He walks downstairs, down towards us. His face is expressionless,
  his attire immaculate.

52

CITY CHURCH.

Organ music as the worshippers come out into the street.

Among the worshippers, distinguished by his loose-flowing cloak
  and his florid clothing, is Rock.

With him are four of his students, including Brown whom last we

saw in Tavern B with Murray and Jennie Bailey. Other of the
faces we recognize, too, as having been among those in the
lecture classes.

Many of the worshippers stop outside the church, bow, raise their
hats, gather in groups.

But Rock and his four disciples stride on down the street.

From outside the church we see how the eyes of many worshippers
follow them; and a few black-apparelled heads come whispering
together.

The organ music fades.

53

HILL ABOVE THE CITY.

Rock and the students are walking up the Hill.
They stop. They look down at the City.
Rock sits on the grass, and the students sit at his feet.

> BROWN. Did you ever hear such a mealy-mouthed sermon,
> sir? It made me . . .
>
> ROCK. Indeed? In my student days I fancied myself as
> something of a sermon-taster, but I cannot say that I was
> ever actually ill from it. I grew accustomed to the taste:
> a not too unpleasant mixture of boiled brimstone and the
> day before yesterday's sprouts. . . .
>
> FIRST STUDENT. What was the sermon about? The
> Sanctity of Human Life, was it? I went to sleep.
>
> ROCK. To sleep, Mr. Duncan? I would not have known.
> You seemed to me to be wearing the same expression of
> studious concentration that you wear in my Anatomy classes.
> How strange and beautiful the City looks to-day. A city
> where good men walk in dignity and peace, and children
> play in green places, and girls are both pure and merry, and
> the hearts of young men are lifted with the aspirations of
> love, and scholars labour diligently with no other motive

49

than the advancement of the knowledge and happiness of mankind. Dear me! Who would think that that lovely City below us is a Gibraltar of propriety and mediocrity, where the good men starve or are hounded into the dark, and the worthless thrive, and the scholars think only of material rewards, and the girls are born with their noses snobbed in the air and their eyes searching for a marriage bargain, and the young men's hearts are lifted only by the thought of easy success. And who would think, too, that within that Gibraltar lies an *inner* island of active evil. . . .

BENNET. [Slowly.] Yes. The Sanctity of the Human Body and the Human Soul. That's what the sermon was about, sir. It's my opinion that . . .

ROCK. Ah! An opinion! Gentlemen, what priceless treasure is to be revealed to us now. . . .

BENNET. [Blushing, and very confused.] I was only going to say, sir, that I haven't got much of an opinion about it anyway. . . .

ROCK. [To the others.] What did I tell you? A treasure! 'My opinion is that I have no opinion.' Excellent! . . . But let us talk about other things. . . .

That Rabelaisian *raconteur,* Mr. Bennet, shall tell us some disreputable stories of his early youth.

And the very young Mr. Bennet is confused again.

DISSOLVE to

Rock and students walking downhill.
Music.
Gathering darkness.
At the foot of the hill, Brown and Students One and Two part from Rock and Bennet.
We see them in *LONG SHOT.*
We hear none of their words, but only the evening music.

MARKET-PLACE.

Music.

Darkness gathering deeper.

The lights are coming on. Lights in the windows of the taverns, and tallow-sticks flaring at the alley corners and outside a few of the Market houses.

But the ordinary life of the Market does not cease with the dark and the coming on of the lights. Children still play on the cobbles; and from the alleys behind them, in the unseen courts and closes, come the voices of other children. And men and women stand about in shop and house and tavern doorways, drinking, talking, quarrelling. And a horse and cart rumble out of darkness, over the cobbles, and into darkness again.

We see Rock and Bennet walking through the Market, towards us.

And we see, too, the crippled boy with the idiot smile (whom we first saw in Sequence 2) playing among a little crowd of children.

He runs away from the children, over to Rock.

And Rock stops, and smiles at him.

> ROCK. Good evening, Billy.

Billy smiles back delightedly, and bobs his head up and down.

> ROCK. It's a cold night to be running about in the streets. . . .
> BILLY. Not for Billy Bedlam. . . . Not cold. . . . [And, like a taught parrot, he gabbles.] He's never cold in September or November or December. . . .
> ROCK. [Patiently.] Why, Billy?
> BILLY. Because there's an ember in the month. . . .

Rock puts money gently into Billy's hand.

> ROCK. Here's a present for you, boy. Hold it in your hand. Don't lose it.

Rock and Bennet walk on.

We hear, from behind them, Billy's voice crying:

BILLY'S VOICE. Night . . . night . . . Doctor Rock. . . .

And we move with Rock and Bennet through the night-time Market.

ROCK. Now he'll hurry as fast as he can on his bent bones to the nearest tavern, and fuddle his few poor wits, and crack his crazed little jokes half remembered from the cradle. . . . Oh, how the pious would lift their hands to heaven to think of a man giving money to an idiot so that he could get drunk and be warm and happy for an hour or two. Let him rather die a sober frozen idiot in the gutter! . . . Would you care to join me at dinner, sir? . . .

BENNET. Thank you, Doctor. . . .

ROCK. Don't call me Doctor. Do I call you Student? Come on, sir. . . .

And they walk out of the Market into:

55

ALLEYWAY.

Rock and Bennet walk on down the Alley, away from us, into darkness.

And we *TRACK UP* the Alley towards a doorway with a tallow-stick burning above it.

Two figures stand in the doorway: a man and a woman.

And coming closer to them, we see that they are Murray and Jennie Bailey.

They are very close together.

They stand, their faces half illuminated and half shadowed by the burning tallow-stick, as though in a little island surrounded by a sea of darkness.

And from that sea come the cries of children at play in the dark; though far off now.

JENNIE. It's good night. . . . good night at the door again. Parting like strangers. . . .

MURRAY. You're close to me for a moment. . . .

JENNIE. Is a moment enough for you, then, my dear, my dear?
And all the long night to go. . . . You're a sad, strange
boy, saying you love me and leaving me all alone. . . .

MURRAY. It's I'll be all alone. . . .

JENNIE. Draw a pretty picture of me, then, to carry about
with you so that you'll never be alone, and put it under
your pillow at nights like a girl puts a lock of hair or a bit
of weddin' cake to wish her sweetheart will come to her. . . .

MURRAY. I couldn't draw *your* picture, Jennie. You're never
the same for a single minute. [Softly.] But you're always
beautiful. I *know* you now; but sometimes I don't know
you at all—when you're gay and *hard* and drinking and
dancing. . . . And not caring. . . . It's the others that
know you then. . . .

JENNIE. Oh, my sweet, you and your silly—others. . . .
Come inside with me now. . . .

And Jennie opens the dark door beneath the burning tallow-stick.
And we see a little passage-way, lit by a gas-jet. And a curtain at
the end of the passage-way.

And from behind the curtain we hear the voices of men and women.
Jennie stands against the passage light, with the other light bright
about her head.

MURRAY. No. No, Jennie. Good night.

And he kisses her, and turns away quickly.

And she steps into the passage-way, and closes the door as the voices
behind the curtain rise. . . .

56

DINING-ROOM OF ROCK'S HOUSE.

From the angle of the door we see that under the light of the high,
many-branched candlesticks sit Rock, Bennet, Annabella, and
Elizabeth.

We *TRACK UP* to the table.

They are drinking coffee, but there is a decanter at Rock's elbow. Annabella is frigidly angry.

ANNABELLA. . . . And that is what I *believe*, and that is what is right. . . .

ROCK. [Pointedly to Bennet.] Have some brandy. . . .

ANNABELLA. There can be, and there always has been, only *one* path of virtue.

ROCK. Surprisingly I agree with you, Annabella.

ANNABELLA. Then it is only for the second time in your life.

ROCK. I can't remember the first. But I agree with what you say, not with what you *mean*. *I believe in the virtue of following no path but your own, wherever it leads.* . . .

ANNABELLA. And that is precisely the sort of statement that antagonizes you to the whole of the profession. . . .

For all your great successes and your famous friends, you do not know how many people there are who would be delighted to see you ruined. . . .

ELIZABETH. [To Bennet.] Do you like this City, Mr. Bennet, after the Continent? I think you were very fortunate to have travelled around so much with your parents in the holidays. . . .

BENNET. I like France, ma'am, very much indeed. Of course, I like this City, too. . . .

ANNABELLA. Mr. Bennet, do you, as a student, find that my brother's language and attitude are congenial to the other students?

ROCK. How d' you find the brandy, Bennet? Not mellow enough for you?

BENNET. No, sir . . . it's . . . excellent. Yes, Miss Rock, we all find Doctor Rock's language and . . . er . . . attitude . . . most . . . congenial and, and . . . and *stimulating*.

ANNABELLA. Like brandy on persons of weak health, physical or mental.

ELIZABETH. I should very much like to see Paris, Mr. Bennet. . . .

ANNABELLA. My dear Elizabeth, is this a geographical con‑
versazione? I merely wanted to know . . .

ROCK. [To Bennet.] Without embarrassing you further,
and allowing you no opportunity of savouring, let alone
swallowing, the brandy you were kind enough to call
excellent, may I explain to you that what my sister really
wishes to know is whether you agree with her that the
medical profession, with some notable exceptions, consider
me a seducer of youth and an atheist? [In another tone.]
You have no need to answer, of course. . . . [Gently.]
Has he, Elizabeth, my dear? I would far prefer to talk
about Paris. . . .

BENNET. [In an agony of embarrassment, but still determined
to defend his master.] I can't pretend to know what the
medical profession thinks of Doctor Rock, Miss Rock, but
we all think that most of the other doctors and professors are
enormously *jealous* of him. [To Elizabeth.] Jealous be‑
cause he's a great anatomist, ma'am, and a great——
[He breaks off.]

ROCK. H'm! I know Paris well, especially the cafés. I
always used to wear a yachting cap in France, I can't think
why. . . . I wish you'd been there with me, my dear. . . .

DISSOLVE to

57

SMALL ROOM IN LODGING‑HOUSE.

Nelly, at the fire, is stirring a wooden spoon in a black pot, and
something is being fried. We hear the sizzling.

Kate, with an almost bristleless broom, is brushing the broken glass
into a corner.

The broken table has been laid: there are four pewter mugs on it.

Suddenly there is a noise of singing and stamping from outside.

The door is crashed open and Broom dances in, a bottle under
each arm.

He winks and leers at the women, nods and jerks his fingers at the open door.

And in through the door Fallon staggers, singing, with a little old woman hanging, half falling, on his arm. She too is trying to sing.

> FALLON. And look what I've brought home, my doves. A pretty old woman with nowhere to sleep . . . have you, Granny? Nowhere to sleep but with us. Shall we give her a bed?
>
> NELLY. Where d' you find her?

Broom is opening a bottle and pouring whisky into the mugs. He gives the Old Woman one.

> BROOM. Drink with Broom!
>
> FALLON. She was lying in the gutter like an old cabbage, weren't you, Granny? Her poor grey hairs dragging in the mud. And who should pick her up but kind Bob?

Fallon lifts the Old Woman up and places her on the bed.

> FALLON. There. The place of honour. Nothing's too good for her.
>
> KATE. What you're going to do?
>
> BROOM. Do? Drink!
>
> FALLON. Do? Drink with Granny. All night long.

The Old Woman titters and drinks. She nearly falls off the bed, but Fallon catches her and lays her down gently.

> FALLON. [Softly.] No harm must come to you now. You might have bumped your head. Then what'd the doctors think?

Broom skips over and takes the Old Woman's mug from her hand and pours whisky down her throat.

She coughs and gasps.

> FALLON. [In a different voice, to the women.] You two be running off on an errand.

Broom points at the Old Woman who is now almost unconscious, spread on her back, her black mouth open.

BROOM. You needn't be long.

FALLON. [Slowly.] Go now.

And the women, without a word, and without looking at the Old
Woman, fasten their shawls and go out.

FALLON. [To the Old Woman, as though to a child.] Up
you get, dear. Don't you want no more whisky? [Into
her ear.] Whisky, whisky!

And, trembling, the Old Woman manages to regain some conscious-
ness. As soon as she does, Broom, ready all the time, pours more
whisky down her throat.

She falls back.

FALLON. Give me the bottle.

Broom hands it to him. Fallon drinks from it. He passes the bottle
back. He rubs off the sweat from his forehead. He moves,
unsteadily, but heavily, to the head of the bed.

And Broom crouches at the foot.

From above, we look down on to the Old Woman's face.

Her eyes open.

Suddenly her face is frightened.

58

CITY SQUARE.

We see Fallon and Broom through the grille in the door of Rock'
Academy, as through prison bars.

Fallon carries the tea-chest.

Now, from behind Fallon and Broom, we see the door opened by
Tom.

We follow Fallon and Broom as they enter the Hallway.

59

HALLWAY OF ROCK'S ACADEMY.

Without any need for instruction from Tom, Fallon and Broom
move with the tea-chest into the Cloak-room under the stairs.

As they go in, so Murray, in evening dress, comes down the stairs and sees them.

In the Hallway he beckons Tom over to him.

> MURRAY. Who are the dapper gentlemen?
> TOM. Bob Fallon and Broom, sir. They're new hands . . .
> but they're getting pretty regular. They ask for ten pounds.

Murray goes into the Cloak-room and comes out a moment later. He nods his head.

> MURRAY. That'll do.

Now, from the back of the Hallway, at the foot of the stairs, we see Tom opening the door wide to Murray.

In the street outside we see a stationary coach.

> MURRAY. [At the door.] If any more bodies call, tell them
> I'm at the theatre with Doctor Rock. Good evening, Tom.

And we see him, in *LONG SHOT* from the back of the Hallway, walk out, down the steps, and into the coach.

60

VESTIBULE OF THEATRE.

At the door leans Jennie Bailey, with a gay shawl round her shoulders.

We see, outside the Theatre, coaches waiting.

There is a great burst of applause, and she turns round to look towards the door of the auditorium.

The audience pours out.

Down the stairs at the side come Rock, Elizabeth, Green, Murray, and Annabella.

From Jennie's angle we see them stop to talk to other members of the audience.

We see Murray looking round him.

We see Hocking.

TRACK UP close to Rock's party.

> HOCKING. Good evening, Doctor Rock.
> ROCK. Good evening, Doctor Hocking.

HOCKING. I do not often see you at the play . . .

ROCK. No, sir. I am able to find my entertainment else-
where. The City is full of low comedians: it is a pity that
the lowest of them all should also be a surgeon. Good night.

And Rock takes Elizabeth's arm, and leads his guests out.

The last of the party is Murray. He sees Jennie Bailey, and stops as
the others walk out to the waiting coaches.

He looks round him quickly, then whispers to her, and hurries
after the others.

Coaches drive off.

And Jennie goes out, too.

We follow her through the darkness until the Theatre lights behind
us fade.

DISSOLVE to

61

MARKET-PLACE.

Night.

We see the entrance to Tavern B from which light and voices pour
on to the cobbles.

Jennie Bailey comes out of darkness into the light and into the tavern.

62

INTERIOR OF TAVERN B.

The tavern is crowded.

Many of the faces are familiar to us now: That old bag of female
bones over there, she was the one who described to Fallon and
Broom the profession of Andrew Merry-Lees; that fat woman
with a pipe there, who tosses down her drink as a tamed seal
swallows a fish, she was the one who kept the stall where Fallon
and Broom bought clothes for their women; that humpback there,
looking at everything with an idiot smile, he is the one called
Billy Bedlam; one of those two very young men over there, being

wise and waggish to a pretty girl of sixteen, is the student Bennet;
that tall man in a scarecrow's top-hat, hiccuping solemnly, he is
the one called Andrew Merry-Lees; and there are others we have
seen before, in the tavern, in the street, in the Market, all of them,
in their way, vice-residents of the tavern; and among them a few
honest, very poor people.

We see all this through Jennie Bailey's eyes.

A dark, pretty young woman with a sulky expression, seated at the
far end of the room, waves her hand.

And from her view we see Jennie Bailey, in her gay shawl, charming
her way down the room, being familiar with every one (including
Billy Bedlam) and over-familiar with some.

Now we see that Jennie Bailey is sitting next to the dark young
woman.

And now we see them very close.

Jennie drinks from the dark girl's drink.

> JENNIE. I been to see the play in the theatre, Alice.
> ALICE. You didn't see no play, dear. You been up High
> Street.
> JENNIE. I did. From the outside. Who shall we get to
> buy us a drink?

She roves her eye round the pub. She nods towards Billy Bedlam.

> JENNIE. Him?

She nods towards Andrew Merry-Lees.

> JENNIE. Him? Oooh, no!

She nods towards Bennet. He catches her glance, is about to blush,
then, remembering his age, winks back.

> JENNIE. Him!

She smiles at Bennet, beckons him over. He comes over.

> JENNIE. Going to buy us some medicine, Doctor?
> BENNET. Oh, of course I am, Jennie. . . .
> JENNIE. Some for Alice and some for me? It's a cold night
> for poor working girls like us. . . .

Bennet goes off.

60

JENNIE. I saw my Doctor at the theatre.   In my box.
ALICE. John Murray?

Jennie nods.

ALICE. Why d' you treat the poor creature so badly, Jennie?
JENNIE. Oh, but Alice darling, I'm so very very fond of
    him. I like him better than any man in the whole world. . . .
ALICE. Then why d' you carry on in front of his eyes and . . .
JENNIE. Oh, but I don't, I don't. . . .
ALICE. . . . and teasing him that he's a parson's son, and
    letting him see you walk out with any Tom, Dick, and
    Harry. . . .
JENNIE. . . . I don't know any Harry. . . .
ALICE. . . . No one could know you loved him, you're so
    brazen, dear. . . .
JENNIE. Oh, I want some fun before I die. . . . You're a
    parson's daughter yourself. . . . He must love me for what
    I am, that's all there is. . . .

Bennet comes back with two mugs.

JENNIE. There, you can always tell, he's got a sweet face.
    . . . I *do* like students and doctors and . . .
ALICE. . . . butchers and bakers and candlestick-makers. . . .

We hear a high yelping laugh, and then Fallon's voice.

FALLON'S VOICE. And there's my darling Jennie. . . .
BROOM'S VOICE. And mine, and mine!

And Fallon and Broom stagger to the table, pushing Bennet aside.
Fallon pulls a bottle out of his pocket.

FALLON. Who's going to share a bottle with two county
    gentlemen?

Fallon and Broom sit themselves next to Alice and Jennie, Fallon
next to Jennie, Broom to Alice. Fallon pulls two mugs across
the table, and fills them.

JENNIE. I never drink with strangers except on Mondays. . .
FALLON. And it's *Monday* to-night.

O the stars are shining, the bells are chiming, we'll drink to Monday and Tuesday and . . .

Fallon pours out another drink.

> JENNIE. And I never drink twice with strangers before twelve o'clock. . . .
> FALLON. And Lord, it's *after twelve*.
> O the moon is singing, the grass is growing. We'll drink to twelve o'clock . . . and one o'clock . . . and two o'clock. . . .

QUICK DISSOLVE to the same table with more mugs and bottles on it.

Fallon and Jennie are now very tipsy.

Broom is smiling, leering, giggling, and clowning to Jennie.

Alice still remains comparatively sober, and still sulky.

> FALLON. [Wheedling.] I got two more bottles in my little room, Miss Pretty Bailey. Two great bottles of dancin' dew that 'll make you think the sun's shining in the middle of the night . . . and satiny shining couches for all the kings and queens to be lying on. . . . And . . .
> ALICE. We're not going.
> JENNIE. Will you give me a diamond ring and a golden bracelet and . . .
> FALLON. I'll give you a bucketful of pearls. We'll sing and dance. We'll be merry as crickets in Rag-and-Bone Alley. . . .
> JENNIE. [Half laughing, half singing.] We'll be merry as crickets in Rag-and-Bone Alley. . . .
> ALICE. [In an angry whisper to Jennie.] You're not going with these two creatures. . . . You must wait for John Murray. . . . Don't drink any more with that Bob Fallon. . . .
> BROOM. And I'll cook you liver and lights. . . .
> JENNIE. Will you cook a partridge for me? . . .
> FALLON. And I'll put a peacock's feathers in your hair. . . .
> JENNIE. Oh, listen to them both. . . . You'd think they

were great rich men with crowns and palaces, not a couple of naughty tinkers. . . .

ALICE. We 're not going. . . .

QUICK DISSOLVE to

63

MARKET-PLACE in the dim moonlight.

Four figures move through the Market: Fallon, Jennie, Broom, Alice. Fallon and Jennie are singing.

FALLON AND JENNIE. We 'll be merry as crickets in . . .

And Broom accompanies their singing, like a dog baying at the moon. Now they are moving through:

64

RAG-AND-BONE ALLEY.

Their singing wakes up a shape that is lying in a dark doorway. Slowly, awkwardly, it rises to its feet. It is Billy Bedlam. He follows the four, with his eyes, down the Alley, and sees them enter the Lodging-house.

65

Darkness.

Fallon, Jennie, and Broom singing and baying in the darkness.

A door is flung open.

We see, for a moment, the small room of the Lodging-house. Nelly stands there at the dead fire.

Then Fallon and Jennie and Broom and Alice stumble into the light of the room.

Fallon lurches over to the table, opens a bottle with his teeth.

He makes an unsteady bow, offers the bottle to Jennie. . . .

FALLON. You first, my Jennie, my merry, my cricket. . . .

Jennie drinks.

Alice looks round the room with fear and revulsion.

Broom leaps on to the bed.

Nelly stands, drab and cross, before Fallon.

> NELLY. Who told you you could bring your women here,
> you and that mad dog. . . .
>
> FALLON. Now, now, Nelly macushla, we've come to sing
> and drink. . . .

But Nelly rushes across to Jennie and pulls the bottle from her lips.

> ALICE. [Urgently.] I told you not to come, Jennie Bailey.
> . . . Let's go, let's go!
>
> FALLON. My Jennie's not going, she's not going, any one
> else in the wide world can go, not Jennie.
>
> ALICE. Come on, Jennie, come on.

But Jennie is sitting, swinging her legs, on the table, and is trying
to open the other bottle.

> FALLON. If you don't like it here, go to your own pigsty.

Alice looks at Jennie, but Jennie has opened the bottle and is
pouring from it into a glass.

And Alice goes. She slams the door behind her.

> NELLY. And *she* goes, too.

Nelly, still with the one bottle in her hand, tries to tear the other
bottle from Jennie.

Fallon suddenly lifts a glass and throws it in Nelly's face.

As she staggers, he takes the bottle from her. She puts her hand up
slowly to her face, and feels the running blood.

And she goes out of the room like an old woman whipped.

Fallon takes Jennie's glass, drinks from it, puts it back in her hand.

And Jennie drinks, swinging her legs.

And Broom is dog-creeping on the floor. As Fallon and Jennie
drink he slips off the buckles from her shoes and leaps, lightly and
silently, to his feet, and is out of the room, closing the door with
no sound.

And Fallon's hand, as he looks at Jennie, slowly drops, and the drink
from the bottle he is holding runs over her dress and down her legs.

DOORWAY IN ALLEY (as in Sequence 55).

Alice is talking excitedly to a woman in the doorway.

The woman nearly fills the doorway. She is dressed in a long, loose shift. Her huge arms are bare.

> ALICE. And I tried to tell her, Rosie, but she wouldn't listen, she was laughing and drinking with him. . . . Oh, I didn't like the looks of him, Rosie. . . .
>
> ROSIE. Go and fetch her back.

Rosie has a voice deep as a man's, and heavy, and slow.

> ALICE. But I 'm telling you, Rosie, he 's no good, he 's like an *animal*; won't you send someone back with me? . . .
>
> ROSIE. Go and fetch her back. There 's persons waiting for her here. . . .

Alice turns away.

67

Darkness.

The pattering of footsteps in the darkness.

A door is flung open.

We see into the small room of the Lodging-house.

But we see no one there.

Then Alice runs in, looks round. She sees Fallon lying stretched on his back on the straw bed in the corner.

> ALICE. Where 's Jennie?
>
> FALLON. [In a dulled voice.] Jennie? She went a long time ago.
>
> ALICE. Where did she go?
>
> FALLON. She went out.

And Alice runs out of the room, leaving the door open.

Alice is running down Rag-and-Bone Alley in the moonlight.
A dark shape leans against a doorway.
Alice stops.

     ALICE. Which way did Jennie go?

Billy Bedlam shakes his head.
Alice points up the Alley.

     ALICE. Did she go that way?

He shakes his head, and stretches out his hand.

     BILLY. Have some snuff. . . .

But Alice runs on up Rag-and-Bone Alley.

69

SMALL ROOM IN LODGING-HOUSE.

Fallon is still lying on the straw bed.
The door is still open.
Nelly comes in. The blood has dried on her cheek. She looks
   round the room.

     NELLY. Where's Jennie?

He puts his hand down at his side, the side nearest the wall, and
   drags up Jennie's gay shawl, and holds it up to Nelly.
His face is hot and wet.

FADE OUT.

FADE IN

70

CITY STREET.

Broad daylight.
Music and the ringing of church bells.
Fallon and Broom walking up street away from camera.

Fallon is carrying a sack on his back.   Broom is holding the end of
  the sack mock-solemnly like a man at the end of a coffin.
We see, as they move, children coming out of the doorways,
  children scampering away from their play to sing and cry together:

> CHILDREN'S VOICES. You 've got a body in the sack!
>> Body-snatchers!
>> Dead!
>> Dead!
>> Dead!
>> Body-snatchers!

And they dance around the sack.
And Broom snaps his teeth at them.
Fallon and Broom walk on.   The voices fade behind them.

DISSOLVE to

7I

CLOSE SHOT of the sack on a table.
TRACK BACK to see that the table is in the Dissecting Room of
  Rock's Academy.
There are many students. Some, with their backs to us, are bent
  over the tables, cutting, probing, snipping. We see their movements but not the objects upon which they are working. Some
  of the students are talking together. None of them takes any
  notice of the sack.
Murray comes in and walks up to the sack.

> MURRAY. [Casually.] Let 's see what we 've got to-day.

He begins to untie the thick ropes about the sack.
Several students gather around him.

> MURRAY. An old trull of eighty with bow legs and a belly
>   like a Lord Mayor's, eh? A tramp from the gutter with
>   cirrhosis of the liver and three teeth? What 's your guess?
>   . . . An old . . .

He opens the neck of the sack, and begins to draw the sack down
  from the head.

Suddenly he stops talking. We see what he sees: Jennie's long fair hair. Slowly he draws the sack down from the face, but we do not see it. The students, silent now, gather around it, and we see only their backs and the profile of Murray. We see that his face has hardened and become grim, his lips are held very tightly together, as though he were forcing himself not to utter a word.

 BENNET. [In a long-drawn-out half-sighing whisper.] God!
 FIRST STUDENT. Here, let me look.

The First Student bends closer over the table.

 FIRST STUDENT. It's Jennie Bailey.
 SECOND STUDENT. Sweet Jennie Bailey.
 BENNET. [Softly.] Yes, it's Jennie! I saw her last night in the Market. . . . She was *singing*. . . .

But Murray does not utter a word.

 THIRD STUDENT. How did she die? . . .
 BENNET. She was *singing* . . . and *dancing*. . . .

Suddenly Murray turns away and strides out of the room.
The students still stand around the body that we do not see.

72

Out in the HALLWAY Murray strides across to the door of the small Cloak-room.

The door is open. Beyond it is darkness. Murray calls into the darkness.

 MURRAY. Tom!

And from the darkness we hear Tom's voice:

 TOM'S VOICE. Coming, sir.

Tom comes out of the darkness like an underground animal. He blinks at the light.

 TOM. Yes, sir? I was . . . cleaning up.
 MURRAY. Who brought the subject in?
 TOM. In the sack, sir? That was Bob Fallon and Broom. . . . Wasn't it fresh, sir?

Murray turns away abruptly and, without a word, goes upstairs.
Now we see Murray walking along the Corridor.
He opens a door and strides in.

73

We see Murray stride into the REFERENCE LIBRARY.
Rock is standing at a bookshelf at the far end of the room, his back
   to us and to Murray.
He turns round as Murray comes in.

> ROCK. You knock at the door very softly, Mr. Murray.

Murray closes the door, and stands with his back to it.
Rock stands with *his* back to the bookcase. Murray speaks slowly,
   deliberately, like a man with a passionate temper who is afraid to
   lose control of it.

> MURRAY. They've got Jennie Bailey downstairs.
>
> ROCK. Indeed? Jennie Bailey? Oh yes, I think I remember
> the name. A beautiful slut with a bold eye and a tongue
> like a drunken horse-thief's.
>   And what might she be doing downstairs? I am sure,
> Mr. Murray, that she is an expert in Anatomy, but her
> knowledge would be too specialized. . . . Or has she come
> merely to entertain?
>
> MURRAY. She has come, sir, to be dissected.
>
> ROCK. How very generous of her. I did not think that
> science was so near her heart. Does she wish to be dissected
> *alive*?
>
> MURRAY. She is dead.
>
> ROCK. That is carrying scientific generosity to its furthest
> limit.
>
> MURRAY. She was murdered.
>
> ROCK. [Sharply.] Who says so?
>
> MURRAY. She was murdered.
>
> ROCK. Are there signs of violence upon the body?

MURRAY. She was murdered by two paid thugs of yours:
Fallon and Broom. I saw her last night after the theatre.
She was well and gay. There are no signs of violence
upon her body.

ROCK. Thugs of *mine*, Mr. Murray? Do you remember that
you yourself paid them for the last *three* subjects?

MURRAY. She was murdered. I saw her. [Slowly, remem-
beringly.] She had a red shawl on.

ROCK. Indisputable evidence that she was murdered. She
should have worn a white shawl, for purity. And what
if she *was* murdered, Mr. Murray? We are anatomists, not
policemen; we are scientists, not moralists. Do *I, I,* care
if every lewd and sottish woman of the streets has her throat
slit from ear to ear? She served no purpose in life save the
cheapening of physical passion and the petty traffics of lust.
Let her serve her purpose in death.

MURRAY. You hired Fallon and Broom to murder her as you
hired them to murder the others.

ROCK. I need bodies. They brought bodies. I pay for
what I need. I do not hire murderers. . . .

Rock walks over to the door. Murray still has his back to it.
Rock stops. Their eyes meet. Then Murray moves aside. Rock
opens the door and walks out. We see him walking down the
Corridor.

74

CUT. DISSECTING ROOM OF ROCK'S ACADEMY.

Rock walks in.

Students are gathered round the table where Jennie's body lies. We
do not see the body.

The students move aside as Rock enters.

He stands in the middle of the group. For a moment he is silent, his
head held a little to one side, looking down at the unseen body.

Then Rock turns away from the table.
Murray stands at the door.

> ROCK. Oh, Mr. Murray. I think that before the body is
> put into the brine bath, a drawing should be made of it.
> Shall we not allow posterity to share our exhilaration at the
> sight of such perfect physical beauty?
>
> I should be much obliged if you yourself would perpetuate
> on paper the loveliness of this poor clay, Mr. Murray. We
> know your skill with the pencil. God should have made
> you an artist. He did the next best thing: he gave you a
> very vivid imagination.

And Rock walks out of the Dissecting Room.
Murray does not move.
The eyes of the students are upon him.

75

A CITY STREET IN THE FASHIONABLE AREA.

Daylight.
Music.

Fallon and Broom are walking slowly up the middle of the street
    towards us, looking all around them with a nudging delight.
Broom wears a new extravagant cravat, but still keeps to his ruffian's
    coat.
Fallon has tied a gipsy-coloured kerchief round his neck.
We do not hear any of the street noises. This is a brief, silent
    scene, to music.
People are walking past them, up and down the street. An elegant
    old lady goes by. Broom side grins, points his finger after her.
A nursemaid with two children passes on their other side. And
    Fallon wags his head in their direction. For their own enjoyment,
    with winks and nudges, they point out in dumb show various of
    the passers-by, especially the elderly and the very young.

DISSOLVE to

76

Murray sitting, alone, in the DISSECTING ROOM.
Night.
A drawing block is on his knees.
We see, over his shoulder, the drawing on the block.
It is a half-finished drawing of Jennie Bailey, lying as though asleep.
   Murray goes on drawing. Now, on the paper, we see take shape
   one arm that hangs over the edge of the table, over the edge of
   her last bed.
Now Murray is drawing the clenched hand of the hanging arm.
And from the picture we *TRACK UP* towards the real hand.
And suddenly the hand unclenches itself: an after-death jerk of the
   nerves.
And two pennies fall out of the now open hand, and drop on to the
   floor. We see them roll along the floor.

77

LARGE LODGING-ROOM.

Nelly and Kate are tidying the room, sweeping dirt into corners,
   covering up tousled beds with mud-coloured blankets, stopping
   to drink from a bottle on the broken table in the centre of the room.
We hear, from outside, the sound of a knock on the door.
Kate wipes her lips on her shawl and tucks the bottle inside her
   cabby-like layers of clothes.

   KATE. More lodgers!

She goes out of the room by the far door.
Nelly tipsily tidies herself, spits in her hand to help straighten a
   hanging lock of stiff hair.
And Kate comes back with a big, old, ragged beggar-man shuffling
   behind her, all dirt and hair, like a tame, tired, time- and whip-
   and weather-beaten bear.

   KATE. You can sleep in any bed you like dad, for twopence
      a night. Clean and comfy.

72

NELLY. Are you alone?

The Old Man nods his head.

> KATE. All alone in the world? Nobody to care about you
> at all?

The Old Man shakes his head.

> KATE. Ach, isn't it a shame. . . . Nobody to care if you 're
> alive or dead. . . .

Kate looks at Nelly.

> NELLY. Let the old man have his bed for a penny, Kate.

And Kate takes the Old Man's luggage—which is wrapped up in
a handkerchief—and they each hold an arm and lead him over
to the bed near the small-room door: the bed where the other
Old Man died.

78

DINING-ROOM OF ROCK'S HOUSE.

Day.

Elizabeth, in dust-cap and apron, is cleaning the silver.

Suddenly there is the long pealing ring of a door bell. And Elizabeth
puts down her cleaning cloth, hurriedly takes off her cap and
apron, and goes out of the room, leaving the door open.

We hear the opening of the street door, and then the voices of Elizabeth and Murray.

> MURRAY. I hope I am not disturbing you, Mrs. Rock.
>
> ELIZABETH. Come in, please, Mr. Murray. Do you want
> to see Thomas? He's lecturing. Oh, you'd know that,
> of course. My sister-in-law's upstairs. . . .
>
> MURRAY. I want to see *you*, if I may.

And Murray follows Elizabeth into the room.

> ELIZABETH. You shall see me cleaning the silver, then. . . .

She puts on her cap and apron again, and begins to polish the
candlesticks on the table.

ELIZABETH. I thought it might be a stranger at the door.
. . . That's why I had to take my cap and apron off. Miss
Annabella would never forgive me if I went to the door
dressed like this. . . . But it's only you. I needn't have
worried, need I? . . .

MURRAY. I'm afraid that after I tell you what I have to tell
you, you will never want to see me again. . . .

ELIZABETH. [Smiling.] Oh no, no, nothing could be as bad
as that. . . . What has Thomas been doing now? Writing
terrible letters to the papers, or telling all the young men to
put gunpowder under the City Hall?

MURRAY. No, ma'am.

ELIZABETH. *I* don't mind, you know. . . . It's only—some
other people mind. Thomas can write or say anything he
likes: I don't *understand* very much of it. . . . What have you
got to tell me?

MURRAY. [Slowly, deliberately.] I believe that Thomas has
instructed two men called Fallon and Broom to commit
murder and to sell him the bodies.

There is a silence. Elizabeth stands still, half turned away from
Murray. Then:

ELIZABETH. That is a—*horrible* lie. If Thomas hears it . . .
MURRAY. He *has* heard it.

Elizabeth begins again to polish the candlesticks. She still does not
look at Murray.

MURRAY. Yesterday the body of a young woman called
Jennie Bailey was delivered to the Academy by Fallon and
Broom. Less than twelve hours before, I had seen her outside the theatre, alive and well. It is not possible that she
could have died a natural death.

ELIZABETH. Can't people die a 'natural death' in twelve
hours?

And under Elizabeth's calm voice there is a new hardness. There
is a tenseness in all her smallest movements as she cleans and

74

polishes, not turning round. She is, quite suddenly, not a sweet and mild young woman but a protectress and an enemy.

MURRAY. She did not die a natural death.

ELIZABETH. Was this 'young woman' strangled, or stabbed, or shot, or poisoned, or beaten to death?

MURRAY. [In a slow, low voice, as though he had said the words over and over to himself.] There were no marks of violence upon the body. . . .

We see Elizabeth's relief expressed in the relaxing of the tenseness of the muscles of her shoulders. And now she turns round to face Murray.

ELIZABETH. And so you have no proof at all. . . . How could you? Why did you come to me with such a story? You should go to the police. . . .

MURRAY. I believe that she was smothered to death in such a way as to leave no signs. . . . I came to you first, because I want you to tell Thomas that he must go away. At once. Out of the country. I owe him a great deal. I would not care to see him hanged.

ELIZABETH. You are very kind. . . . Have you thought about yourself? Run out now and shout your lies in the streets, and they will lock you up because you are a mad-man. Or run to all the lawyers and justices, and they'll ask you for proof and you won't have any: and they'll lock you up because you bear false witness against your neigh-bour. Or go around in the dark, whispering all the foul things in your own mind to everybody that will listen, and you'll make such a panic and scare that Thomas's school will have to close and all the people who had anything to do with it will be stoned and spat upon and driven out. And you'll never, never, never again be allowed to work in any hospital or any school or anywhere. And nobody will ever speak to you again, or touch you, or be seen anywhere in the world with you. . . .

MURRAY. I have thought of that. I have thought of everything.

ELIZABETH. And if you call Thomas a murderer, everybody will call you murderer, too. They will call you murderer and butcher. . . .

MURRAY. All I know is that if Thomas did not *tell* these men to murder, he bought the bodies *knowing* that they were murdered.

ELIZABETH. I thought Thomas told me that it was one of *your* duties to buy the bodies. Will *that* help you very much when you accuse him? Will you go to the police now? Will you tell people what you 've told me? It will be quite easy for you to wreck your life, and his, and mine! I shan't try to stop you.

MURRAY. What shall I do?

ELIZABETH. Keep quiet. You knew the girl—Jennie Bailey?

MURRAY. Yes.

ELIZABETH. What was she?

MURRAY. She was a girl from the market. . . .

ELIZABETH. Was she pretty?

Murray nods, slowly.

ELIZABETH. I think I remember her if she was the girl out-side the theatre. She was—*beautiful*. You liked her very much?

MURRAY. Yes.

ELIZABETH. I think you liked her so much that when she died you—lost your head. You didn't know what you were doing or what you were saying. Do you under-stand? You *imagined things*. Do you understand?

Annabella comes in.

ANNABELLA. Good afternoon, Mr. Murray. I didn't know any one had called. I see my sister-in-law is entertaining you. . . .

ELIZABETH. Mr. Murray called to see if Thomas was here. He had something to discuss with him. But now he says it doesn't matter. . . . Does it, Mr. Murray?

And Murray looks, without speaking, at the faces of the two women.

76

INTERIOR OF TAVERN B, FROM THE ANGLE OF THE DOOR.

Broom is standing in the middle of the room, looking around him.
There are few customers.

In one corner, alone, wrapped up as though against the cold, we
recognize Alice. She raises her head, sees Broom, clutches her
shawl more tightly round her, and turns her head away to the wall.

And we see Billy Bedlam sitting, also alone, staring at an empty mug
before him.

Broom flicks a coin in the air, catches it in the palm of his hand,
looks down into his palm. Then he crosses to Billy.

CLOSE SHOT of Billy and Broom.

> BROOM. Would you be having a little drink, Billy?

Billy smiles up, trustfully, delighted.

> BROOM. [Without turning from Billy, in a high, loud voice.]
> Two gins. [Then ingratiatingly.] It's you and me could
> drink the sea dry, Billy, and eat the fishes and cuddle the
> mermaids and dance a jig and play the penny whistle
> and . . .

The potman comes up with the drinks. Broom pays as he talks, and
the potman goes off.

They drink them off in a gulp.

> BILLY. I've seen a shark. . . .
> BROOM. [Loudly.] Two gins. [Softly.] You could wrestle
> the shark and toss him over your head like a pound of
> cat's-meat. . . . You're strong, Billy. . . .

The potman comes up with the drinks. Broom pays as he talks,
and the potman goes off.

They drink them off in a gulp.

> BILLY. I know a riddle. . . .
> BROOM. Tell Broom your riddle. . . . Two drinks!
> BILLY. In what month of the year do the ladies talk least?

BROOM. Oh, that's a good one. And what month *would* it be, Billy?

BILLY. The month of February, because there wiz least days in it.

And Broom raises his head and yelps with laughter; and slaps his thigh, and cracks his fingers.

Delighted, Billy splutters and crows.

BROOM. Tell Broom a riddle, Billy . . . another riddle. . . .

Broom beckons over his shoulder in the direction of the bar, then leans close to Billy again.

BILLY. I can tell you a riddle that nobody knows and nobody can guess it. . . .

BROOM. What is it, Billy?

BILLY. Though I black an' dirty am,
An' black as black can be,
There's many a lady that will come
And by the hand tak' me.

Now you can't guess that. . . .

BROOM. Ah no, Billy, I can't guess that fickly one. Who learned you all those fickly guesses?

BILLY. It wiz my half step-mither. Oh, she's a cunning old body! Oh, she's cunning as a kitten when we're all sitting beside her round the fireside. She tells us a million million million funny stories, but I don't remember them all. . . .

Though I am black an' dirty an' . . .

BROOM. It's a tea-kettle. . . .

BILLY. [Almost in tears.] Somebody told you.

BROOM. Well, tell us another, *Royal* Billy. . . .

And he beckons over his shoulder, towards the counter, for more drink, and leans again across the table to listen to Billy.

BROOM. And we'll drink . . . and we'll drink . . . and we'll . . .

And his voice softens and softens until it fades.

78

SMALL ROOM IN LODGING-HOUSE.

Candles in bottles on the table.

We see, in a corner, the pile of old rags and bones. It is far higher than when we last saw it.

Kate lies half on, half off the straw bed near the wall.

Nelly is looking out of the window. The window is open. From outside we hear the squealing of pigs.

The door is flung open.

Broom and Billy lurch in.

Nelly turns from the window.

We hear her whisper:

> NELLY. Not Billy Bedlam!
>
> BROOM. [To Nelly.] Shut the window. The pigs is too loud. It sounds like a killing. . . .

Nelly shuts the window.

> BROOM. And bring out a bottle for Billy. . . .

Billy staggers to a chair in a corner, sits on it, tilts it back on two legs and smiles at Nelly, who is staring at him as she brings out a bottle from a cupboard near the window.

> BILLY. He bought me snuff. . . .

Billy opens his box of snuff. Half of it spills over him. He scrabbles it off his clothes.

And Broom takes the bottle from Nelly and carries it over to Billy and gives it to him and watches him drink.

We see Billy's face as he drinks: drunkenly made beautiful.

But we see only the back of the watching Broom, and he does not turn round as he speaks:

> BROOM. Go round the shebeens and find Fallon. Tell him there's business.

Nelly goes to the door; she looks over her shoulder at Billy.

From her angle we see Billy and Broom's back.

BILLY. He gave me snuff. . . .
  He gave me snuff and whisky. . .
  He promised me a shilling. . . .
BROOM. [Still not looking round.] And a sleep. . . .

And, looking at Broom's back and at Billy, we hear the door close.

81

INTERIOR OF TAVERN A.

CLOSE SHOT of Fallon sitting at a table, a mug before him.
His face is covered with sweat.
And terror looks out of his eyes.
He raises his hands before him, palms upward.   They are trembling.
His lips are moving, but no words come.
TRACK BACK to see Nelly sitting down next to him.

NELLY. Broom says you're to come.

Fallon stares in front of him.

NELLY. He says there's . . . work.
FALLON. [Without turning to her.] My hands have worked
  enough.   There's devils in my hands.
NELLY. It's . . . somebody we know Broom's got there. . . .
FALLON. I've known them all, all of them.   They were my
  brothers . . . and my sisters . . . and my mother. . . .
  [In a horrified whisper.] . . . All dead . . . dead. . . .
NELLY. Hurry up with you. . . . Broom's waiting. . . .

Fallon does not move.

NELLY. You've drunk yourself daft again . . . like when you
  went on your knees in the street, praying and shouting. . . .
FALLON. I wish I was workin' again, on the roads, on the
  canals, anywhere. . . .
NELLY. D' you want us all to starve while you blather and
  weep your eyes out. . . .
FALLON. Starving's better than these . . .

And he raises his hands again . . . and suddenly tautens them.
And Nelly pulls roughly, violently, at his sleeve, and drags him up, and pushes him out of the door into the darkness.

82

SMALL ROOM IN LODGING-HOUSE.

We see the room from the angle of the window.

Billy is still sprawling on the tilted chair in the corner.

Broom leans against the table, arms folded, watching Billy. He leans with his head a little to one side, enjoying the spectacle: a freak admiring a freak show.

Kate is still lying half on, half off the bed, her hand trailed in a puddle on the floor.

> BROOM. [Softly.] And when Mr. Fallon comes back, oh, we'll have fun and singing. . . . It's he's got a voice that'll send you to sleep like your mother's. . . . And oh, the joking and riddles!

PAN ROUND to the door as Broom speaks. Fallon is standing there. Behind him, almost in darkness, we see Nelly.

Fallon stands there at the door with his shoulders back and his head high. There is something almost of dignity about him: something that might suggest he is about to make a sacrifice.

And when he speaks, it is without the usual blarneying whine; a horror that has reached him has deepened the tone of his voice.

> FALLON. [Slowly.] Make Kate go.

Now, from Nelly's angle, behind Fallon, we see Broom move across to the bed in two cat-padded jumps and pinch Kate awake.

She looks round the room, thick with sleep. She sees Billy smiling at every one and no one; she sees the malicious face of Broom above her; she sees Fallon grim in the doorway. And, sober in a second, and frightened, she scrambles to the door.

Fallon does not move; she has to squeeze herself past him, keeping her body as far away from his as she can.

> FALLON. Close the door.

CUT to shot, from behind Billy, over his crippled shoulders, of Fallon at the door and Broom by the bed.

Fallon's eyes are staring straight at us.

> FALLON. [Slowly.] You mustn't be frightened, Billy.

Fallon takes a step forward.

> FALLON. [Slowly.] It'll all be over soon. No more bein' hungry. . . .

Now Fallon, slow as a priest, is moving towards us and Billy.

CUT to shot, from door, of Fallon moving towards Billy, and of Billy's bewildered, but still smiling, face. . . .

> FALLON. [Slowly.] No more . . . cold. . . .

CUT to shot, from Billy's angle, of Fallon moving, as though in procession, down the room.

And behind him, on tiptoes, comes Broom. Now they are almost upon us.

And suddenly we hear the voice of Billy: screaming.

83

OUTSIDE THE DOOR OF THE SMALL ROOM.

Nelly and Kate are standing close to the door.

A little light, as though from one candle, falls on their faces.

Around them, darkness.

The women stand tensed, waiting, close together. And from beyond the door comes Billy's scream.

The scream mounts, breaks, and bursts out again. The crash of a falling chair.

And now it is not a scream that comes from beyond the door but a terrified howling; and with it the sound of a deeper voice: Fallon's voice—the voice of the damned inarticulately praying. And with it the smashing of wood, and glass breaking.

Then one scream destroys all other sounds.

The women put their hands over their ears, press their hands hard.

And the women are rocking slowly to and fro, as though at the side
of a death-bed, as though at a wailing-wall.

Then the scream goes out.

Slowly the women grow still, and they move their hands down.

The door opens.

Light falls upon the white-faced women.

Fallon stands at the door with his back to the room, so that we
cannot see his face or the room behind him.

Fallon raises his hand to beckon the women in.

He turns around, goes into the light.

The women go after him, so that the doorway is never unoccupied
and so that we do not see into the room.

Then the door closes.

FADE OUT.

FADE IN

84

Birds flying over the City roofs.

Morning.

Music.

PAN DOWN from the roofs to the MARKET-PLACE.

As we *PAN*, we hear the voices of children rising.

And children are playing in the middle of the Market.

Then there is the clop-clop of hooves on cobbles. And down the
Market comes a horse and cart.

As the horse and cart approach us, we see that Fallon is driving.

There is a large barrel in the back of the cart. Broom is thumping
the barrel in time to the hoof-beats on the cobbles.

The children scatter as the cart drives down.

And then the horse stops.

Fallon raises a stick and beats the horse.

The horse will not move.

Broom stops his rhythmic thumping on the barrel and stands up.

He shouts at Fallon and the horse in his piercing voice, and the scampering children gather round the cart.

> BROOM. Beat the hide off his back, skin the divil alive. . . .

Fallon beats the horse methodically, as though it were a carpet.

> THE CHILDREN. Skin the divil alive.
> BROOM. Oh, the mule of hell, the stinkin' gob of the knackers' yard, I 'll tear off its tail. . . .
> THE CHILDREN. Tear off its tail, tear off its tail. . . .

Fallon climbs off the cart and tries to drag the horse along by its bridle.

The horse will not move. And as Fallon drags and pulls, so Broom in the cart capers and cries, and so the children in delight caper and cry with Broom.

The people of the Market look on with little interest.

> BROOM. I 'll tear the bit out its mouth. . . . Give me a red-hot poker. . . .
> THE CHILDREN. Red-hot poker, red-hot poker. . . .
> FALLON. [Solemnly.] You 'd think the old mare had risen in judgment against us. . . .

A Porter passes the horse and cart, pushing an empty barrow. He pays no heed to the caterwauling of Broom and the children.

Fallon sees the Porter.

> FALLON. Hi, there!

The Porter stops.

> BROOM. I 'll kick it in the kyte. . . .
> FALLON. Would you take a barrel with you for two shillings? It 's only a little barrel. . . .
> PORTER. Where to? It 's a great big barrel. . . .
> FALLON. My friend 'll show you where.

Fallon beckons Broom, who has now stopped cursing the horse and is snapping like a dog at the children.

> FALLON. Here 's the shillings.

And Fallon, Broom, and the Porter lift the barrel down and put it
on the barrow. As they carry it the Porter says:

>PORTER. What you got in the barrel?
>
>BROOM. Potatoes.
>
>FALLON. Keep your talk in your mouth. You've got your
>money. . . .

And Broom and the Porter go off with the barrow.

And suddenly the horse, as soon as the barrow has gone, goes off
himself down the Market, to the cries of the children, at a brisk trot.
Fallon shouts after it, but it trots on.

>THE CHILDREN. Skin the divil alive. . . . Tear off its tail,
>tear off its tail. . . Kick it in the kyte. . . .

Fallon, after one shout, makes no attempt to follow the horse but
walks back in the direction from which he had come; walks off
heavy-shouldered and heavy-footed, his head sunken.

The voices of the children fade.

85

RAG-AND-BONE ALLEY.

TRACK UP to where a middle-aged man and woman are standing
outside the door of the Lodging-house. The woman carries a
baby in a shawl. The man holds a little child by the hand.
They are dressed like beggars. The man is carrying a bundle in
a stick over his shoulder. He knocks at the door.

>WOMAN. It's a poor, dirty place.
>
>MAN. It's got a roof. . . .
>
>WOMAN. I think I'd rather be on the roads, sleeping in the
>hedge in the cold. . . .

The door opens.

Kate stands in the doorway.

She wears a new shawl.

>KATE. You'll be wanting a bed? They're twopence.
>
>MAN. Bed.

The man unwraps a piece of cloth from his pocket, and brings out a coin.

> KATE. There's nobody sleeping at all here now. . . . You can take your fancy where you sleep. . . .

The man and the woman follow her into the house and into:

The Lodging-Room.

Even in daylight it is half dark. . . .

Kate walks down the room, and the man and the woman follow her.

> KATE. You're strangers here. . . .
> MAN. Strangers everywhere. . . .
> KATE. You're from the roads?

The man nods.

> WOMAN. I think we won't be troubling you for a bed. . . . It's *dark* here. . . .
> KATE. It's darker on the roads. With no one you know in the world, and no one to take care of you. . . . I'll make the beds a penny each. What names d' you go by?
> MAN. Mr. and Mrs. Webb.
> WOMAN. We're respectable people. . . .
> KATE. We're all respectable here. Just my husband and me. He's in the way of a merchant. . . .

The man flings his bundle on a bed. And Kate looks at Mr. and Mrs. Webb.

86

CITY STREET.

The Porter is pushing his barrow along, Broom at his side.

> PORTER. You're sure you said it was potatoes in your—*little* barrel?

Broom winks.

PORTER. They're very heavy potatoes. Where do we go with them?

BROOM. Up the City square. Doctor Rock's Academy.

PORTER. [With a sideways glance at Broom.] He must be very fond of vegetables. . . .

87

HALLWAY OF ROCK'S ACADEMY.

Night.

The Hallway is deserted.

The door to the small Cloak-room under the stairs stands open.

Murray comes out of the Cloak-room.

He looks around him, like a man slowly coming out of a nightmare and trying to grow accustomed again to the familiar things of the daytime world.

MURRAY. Tom! Tom! Where are you, Tom?

But it is only a whisper.

And now he walks up the Hallway past the glass cases slowly.

He opens the door, and walks out through the colonnade into the moonlit garden of City Square. And as he moves through the garden so we hear the voice of his mind, and the remembered voices of others.

MURRAY'S VOICE. Who brought the subject in, Tom? There's no need to ask.

TOM'S VOICE. Fallon and Broom, sir; Fallon and Broom. . . .

MURRAY'S VOICE. What can I do?

ELIZABETH'S VOICE. Keep quiet. . . .

MURRAY'S VOICE. Keep quiet about Jennie or they'll lock you up. . . .

ELIZABETH'S VOICE. Keep quiet. . . .

MURRAY'S VOICE. Keep quiet about Billy Bedlam in the little room, or they'll call you a murderer and a butcher. . . .

ELIZABETH'S VOICE. . . . stabbed or strangled, or beaten to death, or . . .

MURRAY'S VOICE. There are no marks of violence upon the body.

ELIZABETH'S VOICE. . . . You bear false witness. . . .

MURRAY'S VOICE. I swear that Jennie and Billy are murdered. . . .

ELIZABETH'S VOICE. It is quite easy for you to wreck your life. . . .

And he turns and walks back through the garden towards the Academy. Now his step is quicker and more purposeful.

88

ELIZABETH'S ROOM.

Rock, his coat off, but still immaculately dressed, is seated in a deep chair with his head against the back of it.

Elizabeth is curling what remains of his hair with curling-tongs.

Rock has an air of indolent luxury.

ROCK. [Complacently.] The sensual apotheosis of the intellectual animal. . . .

ELIZABETH. If you say so, my dear.

ROCK. The mind is relaxed, the body is pleasured and pampered, rancour has taken a holiday, and I am full of bliss, like a cat on the tiles of heaven. . . .

ELIZABETH. It must be very nice to talk. . . .

ROCK. It is comparable only to the pleasure of not having to think as you talk. . . . [Sighing.] I am a fool to-day.

ELIZABETH. Yes. Thomas . . .

ROCK. [With a change of voice.] But not so much of a fool as some I know. That rumour-breeder of a Murray! Falls in love with a pretty face and then won't cut it up once the little trollop's dead. Says she's murdered. Says, in effect, I murdered her myself.

ELIZABETH. [Mildly.] Oh, Thomas.

ROCK. When I take up assassination, I shall start with the surgeons in this city and work up to the gutter. . . . And

88

now, to-day, along he comes with some fantastic rigmarole
about a crippled idiot. Billy Bedlam. Says *he*'s murdered,
too. Poor Billy's bed was the cobbles, rain or snow, and
he ate like a rat from the garbage heaps, and swallowed all
the rot-gut he could buy or beg. He was a consumptive
and an epileptic. A wonder he hadn't been found dead
years ago. . . .

ELIZABETH. What did you tell Mr. Murray?

ROCK. I said: 'Mr. Murray, go down and cut up the body
and put it in the brine baths. Be careful you don't fall in
yourself—you're wearing a good suit!'

ELIZABETH. [Casually.] And what did he do?

ROCK. What did he do? Why, what I told him to do,
of course. No vicious-minded little prig with emotional
adenoids is going to intimidate *me* with his whine and wail
of 'Murder! Murder!' He suffers from hallucinations.
My hands, to him, are red as Macbeth's. . . .

Rock raises his very white hands in an elegant gesture, and smoothes
the palm of one hand along the back of the other. . . .

89

Music.

Pitch darkness.

Through the darkness, the laughter of Broom.

Then sudden light, and Fallon's hands, palms downwards, fingers
stretched and tautened, murdering down the screen.

As the hands move we hear Fallon's voice, blurred in a distorting
mirror of sound.

FALLON'S VOICE. There's devils in my hands. Let me go,
my hands!

Then, close, from above, the upward-staring faces of old women and
children, their eyes wide, their mouths open.

FALLON'S VOICE. Don't be frightened. . . . There's nothing
to lose. . . .

Then Fallon's hands, palms upwards, fingers damp and limp, trembling up the screen.

> FALLON'S VOICE. It's all lost. . . .

Then *CLOSE-UP* of Fallon's face, drunk, arrogant, grinning.
And we hear a voice questioning the face.

>> VOICE. And where d'you get all the money so quick? You're rich, you're *rich*, you're . . .
>> FALLON'S VOICE. Ach, I done a little smuggling; a little bit o' drink on the sly. . . .

The questioning Voice continues through a *CLOSE-UP* of Nelly in a new feathered bonnet. Nelly drunk, secretive. . . .

>> VOICE. And where d'you get all the money so quick? You're *rich*, you're . . .
>> NELLY'S VOICE. Oh, I've been left a property in the country.

CLOSE-UP of Kate in a new bonnet.

>> VOICE. And where d'you get all the money . . . [The Voice fades.]
>> KATE'S VOICE. Oh, Fallon's the favourite of a great lady. . . . *Twenty* pounds a visit she gives him. . . .

Then *CLOSE-UP* of children's faces.

> VOICE. Where's Billy? Billy Bedlam?

And the voices of the children answer as we see a *CLOSE-UP* of Alice.

>> VOICES OF CHILDREN. Gone, gone . . .
>> VOICE. Where's Jennie? Jennie Bailey?

And Alice's voice answers as we see a *CLOSE SHOT* of a sack put down and hands undoing the sack.

> ALICE'S VOICE. Gone, gone . . .

And out of the undone sack comes a human arm, and we hear the voice of the Porter.

> PORTER'S VOICE. Doctor Rock is very fond of vegetables. . . .

CLOSE SHOT of an Old Man, drooling drunk, his head capsized on one shoulder.

> BROOM'S VOICE. Drink with Broom. . . . Drink. . . .

A hand with a bottle in it stretches across the screen towards him.
CUT to *CLOSE-UP* of the face of an Old Woman looking up at the bottle held across the screen.

> BROOM'S VOICE. Drink . . . drink. . . .

And, loudly, there is the noise of the pigs squealing.

DISSOLVE the picture to

90

INTERIOR OF GROCER'S SHOP.

From the end of the shop, opposite the door, we can see a section of the Market-place in daylight.

The Grocer, behind the counter, is a truculent man in a dirty apron, who seems to have given up hope a long time ago: a man always at the end of his patience.

And before the counter an Old Woman is standing, wrapped in pieces of the discarded clothing of the other poor.

> GROCER. For the last time, I don't know a Flynn. . . .
>
> OLD WOMAN. Timothy Boylan Flynn. . . .
>
> GROCER. I don't know a Flynn, I've never known a Flynn, I never want to . . .
>
> OLD WOMAN. From County Donegal. . . . He came over two years ago and a half. . . . He's a tall, dark boy. . . . The lobes of his ears is pointed. . . .

Fallon comes in at the shop door. He stands, framed against the Market, listening.

> GROCER. 'What's the time of the day?' 'Can you give me a wooden box?' 'My sister's fallen under a hay cart—can you lend me a penn'orth of brandy.' 'Have you seen a Flynn?' Will nobody ever *buy* anything? . . .
>
> OLD WOMAN. Could you spare me a bite o' bread, then?

The Grocer controls himself as Fallon, with a winning smile, comes
to the counter.

> FALLON. [To the Old Woman.] Did I hear you say
> 'Flynn'? That was my mother's name.
>
> OLD WOMAN. From Ardara, Donegal?
>
> FALLON. [Amazed.] Ardara, Donegal! My mother's town!
> And would *your* name be—Flynn, too?
>
> GROCER. *Her* name's Flynn, she's *looking* for a Flynn, and
> now your *mother's* name is Flynn. . . .

Fallon, still looking at the Old Woman, hands an earthenware jug
over the counter to the Grocer.

> FALLON. Fill it up with dew.

The Grocer disappears behind the counter.

> FALLON. [Affectionately to the Old Woman.] Then you're
> my little cousin. . . .

He kisses her forehead. . . .

> FALLON. Cousin Flynn. . . .
>
> Faith, what a day of all days! I'm walking along gay
> as a thrush, I'm fragrant with the sweet smell of money,
> to-night's Hallowe'en when the witches fly and the whisky
> pours like rain, and who should I meet on top of it all but
> a Flynn from Ardara!

The Grocer returns to his place behind the counter; he hands over
the earthenware jug to Fallon. Fallon, tossing coins carelessly on the
counter, pays for it; but he does not take his eyes off Mrs. Flynn. . . .

> MRS. FLYNN. It's my son for I'm looking all over, sir. . . .
>
> FALLON. [Emphatically.] . . . Cousin. . . .
>
> MRS. FLYNN. [Hesitatingly.] . . . Cousin. . . .
>
> FALLON. And we'll find your son for you if we have to pull
> the town down and scramble among the cobbles. . . .
>
> You come with me, cousin . . . you're welcome as sun-
> light. . . . I'll buy you a present for Hallowe'en, and I'll
> take you back to my fine house and we'll kick up a din
> like all Donegal drunk. . . .

Fallon, with the jug and Mrs. Flynn, moves towards the door of the shop, towards the darkening Market.

As they go out we see a *CLOSE SHOT* of the Grocer.

GROCER. [With an awful resignation.] Hallowe'en! . . .

91

RAG-AND-BONE ALLEY.

Late evening.

Music.

The Close is desolate.

We hear the dark noise of the wind blowing.

The noise grows, but the Close is emptily still.

The wind rises, to the rise of music.

And out of the gutters float the wind-driven shapes of witches and demons:

Waste paper flying out of the gutter, eddying into the air, fluttering, as though winged, past the shadowy houses:

Paper and rubbish gusted suddenly from the cobbles to flap and float about the street, to beat against the windows and scrabble there, to rise on the screaming breath of a wind and drift before the Lodging-house:

Straw blown in a squall, straw shapes and garbage shapes puffed through the growing, blowing dark:

Hay wisps and knotted straw, dust clouds and cloth shreds, small crumpled nameless shapes, light as paper and string, scudding through the narrowness:

All the inanimate furies of the Close alive suddenly, crying like the wind through telegraph wires, grotesque dancers from the dirt. . . .

92

Now we are standing at the end of the LARGE LODGING-ROOM.

We are looking down the mostly dark long room and through the open door into the small room.

We hear laughter, and snatches of singing, and a jig tune played on a penny whistle.

Broom and Kate, arm in arm, come dancing out of the small room, turn in the narrow aisle between the beds, and dance, singing, back. We *TRACK UP* slowly to the open door.

As we track we see that one of the beds is occupied: by a baby and a young child. They are the children of Mr. and Mrs. Webb. They are asleep. The child's arm is held protectingly around the baby.

Now we are near the open door.

We see, in the small room, Fallon leaning against the table, playing a whistle. There are cups and mugs on the table, bottles, and the earthenware jug.

Behind Fallon are a man and a woman: a squat and hairy man not unlike Fallon, and a slatternly young woman with wayward hair and smile.

And Broom and Mrs. Flynn, arm in arm, come dancing out of the small room, towards us.

We see them close as they turn in the narrow aisle between the beds.

Mrs. Flynn is gay as an old cat.

Broom is smiling and possessive.

They dance, singing, back into the small room.

We *TRACK* right up to the open door.

In the small room we see that there are nine people: Fallon, penny-whistling at the table; the two strangers behind him singing the words of a jig; Kate and Nelly on the straw bed, beating jig-time on the littered floor; Broom and Mrs. Flynn dancing between the table and the bed, dancing around the table; and Mr. and Mrs. Webb. Mr. Webb, with a look of bemused contentment, is soaking pieces of bread in the earthenware jug and eating them; Mrs. Webb, disapproving, sits on the edge of the one sound chair in the room.

Mrs. Webb complains, through the singing, the dancing, the floor-beating, and the whistling.

 MRS. WEBB. Oh, the noise, it 'll wake all the neighbours. . . .

THE MAN. They wouldn't wake to-night if you set their clothes on fire. . . . All the city's drunk. . . .

MRS. WEBB. [To Mr. Webb.] And stop eatin' bread and gin; it's bad for the stomach.

BROOM. It's Hallowe'en. . . .

THE MAN. It isn't us who's only making the din, you listen now. . . . Shh!

The Man raises his hand. For a moment the room is quiet. The dancers pause. From outside we hear the noise of drunken singing, and voices bawling and brawling.

Then Fallon begins to play again, and Broom and Mrs. Flynn dance again, and the Man and the Woman sing, and Kate and Nelly, speechless on the bed, go on thumping.

MR. WEBB. Bread and gin's good for the stomach.

MRS. WEBB. You'll be waking the children, that's what'll happen next, with your caterwauling and your bang-bangs and your . . .

Fallon stops playing.

FALLON. And can't a man have a party now in honour of his cousin?

MR. WEBB. And rum and spuds is good.

FALLON. [To Mrs. Webb.] You're an auld spoil-sport, Mrs. Webb, you'd stop the dead dancin' on Judgment Day. . . .

The baby, from the next room, begins to scream.

Mrs. Webb jumps up and goes out.

But the screaming continues.

FALLON. Now that's a baby that likes good music. . . .

And he raises his penny whistle and plays again.

Mrs. Webb puts her head round the door.

MRS. WEBB. For the Lord's sake now, is this a lodging house or a wake?

Fallon nods to Nelly.

And Nelly totters to her feet and goes out of the room.

93

In the LARGE LODGING-ROOM we see Nelly and Mrs. Webb at the bed of the screaming baby.

Through the open door we see the singers and dancers.

>NELLY. Oh, the poor creature. It screams like it swallowed a pin. . . . And Fallon 'll be playing his whistle all night . . .

Through the open door we see Fallon whistling and dancing a lonely jig.

>NELLY. . . . and there 'll not be a breath of peace. . . . [Wheedling.] Now why don't you take the children away for the night. . . . Fallon's brother there will give you a bed and a plate of food. . . . And Fallon and us 'll stay singing with old Mrs. Flynn till we a' fall down. . . .

The baby screams louder than ever.

>MRS. WEBB. [Calling through the door.] Come on with ye, Mr. Webb.

Mrs. Webb begins to lift the children out of bed and wrap clothes around them.

94

Through darkness we see a shivering candle move, and moving figures. The baby is still screaming.

>MR. WEBB. I don't want to go out in the cold. . . .
>MRS. WEBB. You and your bread and gin! . . .
>THE MAN. Only a couple of steps from here, Mrs. Webb. . . .
>MR. WEBB. It 's Hallowe'en! . . .
>NELLY. I think you 're very wise to go, my dear. There 's no knowing what pranks Mr. Fallon 'll be up to to-night. . . .

A door is opened.

We see Rag-and-Bone Alley in the moonlight.

And the Man and the Woman, and Mr. and Mrs. Webb and the baby and the child, go out into the moonlight.

And Nelly closes the door.

Pitch darkness. From the darkness a sudden swell of sound: the squealing and squeaking of the tin whistle, and the singing of Broom.

Then momentary quiet.

Then Broom's singing again, and, suddenly through it, a long, high, distant cry dwindling into silence again.

95

Snow falling in hard, bright morning light.

Nothing on the screen but the falling snow. We hear a cock crow.

We CUT to a cock, on a wall, crowing in the middle of the snow, defiantly crying the morning up to the thick, falling flakes.

And now, as the snow drifts and drives past our eyes, we are looking, from the outside, through the Lodging-house window into the small room.

Isolated, behind the shifting wall of snow, sit Fallon and Broom, Nelly and Kate, at the table in the middle of the room. Only Fallon is not eating.

We move through the snow and through the window into the room and towards the table.

We see the details of the room very clearly now in the merciless morning snow-light: no shadows, no twisted shapes in half-darkness, but only the bed with its straw guts straggling out, and the fouled straw-heap on the floor at the foot of the bed, and the thrown-away bottles and the flung scraps of clothes, and the broken glass and the drying pools of drink, and the last and the snippets of leather, and the tin whistle cast near the straw, and the piled boots in the corner, and the iron pot near the smoking fire.

Then Fallon rises from the table and crosses to the window.

From behind him, looking over his tensed shoulders, we see the falling snow.

FALLON. The snow won't ever stop. It's like the last day.

And his voice, and his measured movements, and the concentrated stillness of the others, suggest the anticlimax after death.

97

And now, from the end of the room opposite the door, we see the door open and Mr. and Mrs. Webb come in. Their clothes are white with snow.

Broom leaps to his feet. Fallon turns, with a measured, deliberate movement from the window.

Nelly and Kate sit still at the table, looking up at Mrs. Webb.

> BROOM. [With a frightening smile.] You frightened us.

And he goes out of the room, followed by Kate.

> NELLY. You're early.
>
> MRS. WEBB. I been up and about since dawn; the baby wouldn't fall to sleep at all—it screamed like things were after it. . . .

Fallon stands still at the window, looking at Mrs. Webb.

> NELLY. What have you come for so early?
>
> MRS. WEBB. I come to look for the little boy's stockings. I left them here last night drying by the fire; and I come for our bits and pieces. . . . It's time we're moving. . . .

Mrs. Webb is looking round the room.

She pulls out a clay pipe from her wrappings and lights it at the fire.

With the blackened pipe burning like a little hayrick in her mouth, she bends down and searches among the scraps of clothes on the floor near the straw.

> FALLON. Get away from that straw with your old pipe. . . . You'll have the room blazing. . . .

Fallon speaks so harshly that Mrs. Webb takes an involuntary step backward and sits on the end of the bed.

> MR. WEBB. Where's Mrs. Flynn? [Appreciatively.] She was a very gay old woman, dancin' like a nanny-goat. . . .
>
> NELLY. She was ow'r gay with Fallon. I tumbled her out of the house in the middle o' the night. . . .
>
> MR. WEBB. [With a side look at his wife.] I like a gay old woman. . . .
>
> FALLON. Get out o' my room. . . . Take your reeky scraps of rubbish and your yelpin' children and get out. . . .

Fallon does not move from the window, but his stillness is more
menacing than movement.

And Mr. and Mrs. Webb go out.   As they go Mrs. Webb whines:

>MRS. WEBB. I want my little boy's stockings. . . .

Fallon is alone with Nelly.

>FALLON. The snow's falling heavier.
>The world's cold.

He shivers, pulls his coat closer about him.

>FALLON. It's cold in hell to-day.
>The fires are out.

Nelly looks at him in uncomprehending silence.

>FALLON. Nothing can burn me any more.
>I'm a cold man, Nelly.
>I'm numb all over, like an old dead finger-nail.
>No more dancing.
>No more drinking and singing.

He shivers again, standing against the window and the snow.

>FALLON. I got work to do.

And he goes out, followed by the strangely silent Nelly.

The door closes.

The room is empty.

Then the door opens, very slowly, and Mrs. Webb puts her head
round and looks at the emptiness.

She comes in, whispering over her shoulder.

>MRS. WEBB. They've gone.

And Mr. Webb comes in, nervously glancing behind him and on
every side.

>MR. WEBB. Find the stockings and let's be out of the house.

Mrs. Webb is down on her knees now by the pile of old clothes; she
rummages through them.

>MRS. WEBB. Who wanted to come to this house?   I said
>it was bad.   I could smell the badness as I come in.   It's
>nothing but drinking and howling all night. . . .

99

Suddenly she stops in her scrabbling search through the clothes and lifts up a crumpled dress.

    MRS. WEBB. It's the old woman's dress.

    MR. WEBB. How'd she be walking in the streets in the snow without her dress?

    MRS. WEBB. It's the old woman's dress. I mind the colour.

She starts to search among the clothes again, her hands nearing the straw.

    MR. WEBB. A body doesna walk in the streets without her . . .

Mrs. Webb lifts up a ragged shawl.

    MRS. WEBB. And here's her little patchy shawl. . . .

Now she is worrying the straw, like a dog on a scent.

    MRS. WEBB. And here's her . . .

And Mrs. Webb screams.

A human arm lies naked in the parted straw.

Mrs. Webb springs up and stands, with her back to us, looking down at the straw and the arm.

The scream stops.

Mr. Webb bends down; facing us, he flings the rest of the straw aside.

We do not see what he reveals, for Mrs. Webb stands between us and it.

    MR. WEBB. The gay old woman! Her face is a' slimy.

Music.

Mrs. Webb rushes out of the room.

And, as Mr. Webb follows her, we see, for a flash, the dead white face among the straw.

96

In the LARGE LODGING-ROOM Mr. and Mrs. Webb are frenziedly packing their bits and pieces into a sheet.

The music rises.

They rush, he with the sheet sacked over his shoulder, to the far door.

And suddenly Nelly is standing there, in the doorway.

The music stops.

> NELLY. Where are you going? What have you seen?
>
> MRS. WEBB. Let me out, she's dead. . . .
>
> NELLY. She died in her sleep. . . .
>
> MR. WEBB. Her mouth's blood. . . .
>
> MRS. WEBB. For the love o' Mary . . .
>
> NELLY. *She died in her sleep.* . . .
>
> MRS. WEBB. . . . Let me out. . . .

Nelly tears inside her apron, pulls out a purse, opens it. She pushes a handful of coins towards Mrs. Webb.

> NELLY. Nobody knows her, nobody'll claim her, you mustn't tell a word . . .
>
> MR. WEBB. Stand away . . .
>
> NELLY. . . . she died like a baby. . . .
>
> MRS. WEBB. You killed her in there last night. . . .
>
> NELLY. You musn't tell a word, mercy, quiet, quiet. . . .
> Fallon 'll give you ten pounds, ten pounds a week . . .

Mr. Webb thrusts Nelly aside.

Mrs. Webb runs through the door, Mr. Webb after her.

Nelly, at the door, cries out after them . . .

> NELLY. Ten pounds . . .

97

RAG-AND-BONE ALLEY.

Music.

Snow falling heavily.

Mr. and Mrs. Webb rush out of the Lodging-house.

The Webbs' boy, with the baby in his arms, stands, waiting, like a little snow man near the door.

Mrs. Webb snatches the baby from his arms, hugs it to her shawls, and hurries on up the Alley.

Mr. Webb takes the boy's hand and follows.

They keep to the right of the Alley.

And down the left of the Alley, coming towards the Lodging-
house, we see Fallon and Broom and a Porter.

But, with the fierce snow driving upon them, upon their faces and
their eyes, they do not see the wrapped-up figures of the hurrying
Webbs.

And the Webbs do not see them.

98

SMALL ROOM IN LODGING-HOUSE.

In the middle of the room is a tea-chest.

Fallon, Broom, and the Porter stand, snowy-coated, around the chest.

The Porter is the one we saw taking the barrel in his barrow.

He is pressing down the lid with all his weight.

And Fallon helps him.

Broom points a finger at the top of the lid.

A bunch of grey hair hangs out.

Fallon crosses to the last and the leather pieces and brings back a
pair of cobbler's scissors.

The Porter cuts off the hair with the scissors.

99

INTERIOR OF POLICE STATION.

Mr. and Mrs. Webb are talking to a Policeman.

> MR. WEBB. And there was blood all over her face. . . .
>
> POLICEMAN. Aye.
>
> MRS. WEBB. And her poor lips were blue and her eyes were
> staring out as though somebody'd pressed 'em with his
> thumbs. . . .

The Policeman nods.

> MR. WEBB. She said she came from Donegal. . . .
>
> POLICEMAN. The 'dead woman' told ye she'd come from
> Donegal?

CITY STREET.

We see Fallon and Broom walking, in the slanting snowstorm, by the side of the Porter and his barrow with the tea-chest on it.

INTERIOR OF POLICE STATION.

Mr. and Mrs. Webb are still pleading to the Policeman.

> MR. WEBB. No, no, sir, she said she'd come from Donegal when we was all drinkin' together last night. . . .
> POLICEMAN. Drinkin'!
> MRS. WEBB. Mrs. Flynn her name was, I've told you twenty times. . . .

Mr. Webb, with hesitant, frightened fingers touches his own mouth.

> MR. WEBB. And now there's blood all over here. . . .
> POLICEMAN. [Placatingly.] You sit down now. I'll come with you by and by. . . .

He turns away from them and moves towards the back of the room.

> MRS. WEBB. [Dully, as though repeating a lesson.] Mrs. Flynn her name was. . . . They killed her. . . . Fallon and Broom. . . .

The always shadowy HALL in ROCK'S ACADEMY, with its white secret witnesses staring from the glass cases.

Rock is mounting the stairs.

We follow him as he climbs, and hear the voice of his mind.

> ROCK'S VOICE. Gentlemen. . . . Gentlemen, let us to-day dissect the human conscience. Lay it on the slab. Open it up.

You see? The liver of the conscience is knobbled by emotional excesses.

The veins of the conscience are full of bad blood.

The heart of the conscience palpitates like a snared rabbit's. . . .

Now he is walking along the Corridor, opening a door, to the small Reference Library.

103

REFERENCE LIBRARY IN ROCK'S ACADEMY.

ROCK'S VOICE. In short, gentlemen, the conscience is a *very* unhealthy subject. . . .

And, at the end of these words, he is sitting in a chair behind a desk, facing us.

The room is empty.

And Rock, at the desk, addresses the empty room as though there were a gathering of students in it, turning from one invisible listener to another.

ROCK. There is right and wrong, gentlemen, just as there is right and left. Mine is the *right* direction. The fact that the majority would consider it the *wrong* direction, only substantiates my opinion that I am right. . . .

There is a knock on the door.

ROCK. Stay out.

Tom comes in.

ROCK. I see, sir, that to keep you out I should have said, 'Come in.'

TOM. Fallon and Broom, sir.

ROCK. Indeed? Must I laugh, weep, tear my hair, swoon for ecstasy!

TOM. They've brought a body, sir.

ROCK. I did not expect that they would bring a soul.

TOM. [Suggestively.] They bring so many subjects, sir . . .
    sixteen or more up till to-day . . . and always fresh. . . .
ROCK. They are corpse-diviners. Or, as some have green
    fingers for gardening, so they have black fingers for death.
    Do you expect the dead to walk here, Tom? They need
    assistance. Fallon and Broom provide that assistance.
        Have Mr. Murray pay them.
TOM. Yes, sir.

Tom, with a side glance at Rock, goes out.
And Rock, alone, again speaks in a soft voice to his unseen audience.

ROCK. You see, gentlemen?

104

SMALL ROOM IN LODGING-HOUSE.

We look at the room from above.
In the centre of the room stands the Policeman. Behind him,
    standing close together for protection, are Mr. and Mrs. Webb.
Fallon leans against the table, facing the Policeman.
And behind him are Kate, Nelly, and Broom
They are frozen.
As, from above, we move down closer to them, they unfreeze.

FALLON. [Smiling.] And where did the old fools tell ye
    they saw the body, sir?

Mrs. Webb points to the straw.
The Policeman kicks the straw aside. Broom laughs.

FALLON. Maybe the mice, they dragged it down their little
    hole. . . .

The Policeman bends down, to stare at the floor-boards.

POLICEMAN. Blood on the boards.

A moment's silence.

FALLON. And has there ever been, for the love o' God, a
    Hallowe'en party with no blood spilt? We was all con-
    vivial; there was fightin' in every room of the house.

NELLY. And the old woman Flynn, she was so fashous I told her go with the toe of my boot. . . .

KATE. [Pointing to the Webbs.] And it's they were picking the pockets of the poor innocent persons that couldn't get up from the floor. . . .

NELLY. It's all lies, lies they said. . . .

The Policeman picks up the dress that Mrs. Webb had found.

KATE. Don't you trust them, they're beggars, sir. . . .

BROOM. They eat dead cats. . . .

MRS. WEBB. That's Mrs. Flynn's dress. . . . I mind the colour. . . .

BROOM. Fur and all. . . .

NELLY. That's not hers, it's mine. . .

POLICEMAN. Blood on the front.

NELLY. Fallon hit me with a glass in the face and the cut ran. . . .

MR. WEBB. The old woman's face was a' slimy. . . .

And as Mr. Webb speaks, so we hear the ringing of church bells. . . .

DISSOLVE.

105

Policeman and Mr. and Mrs. Webb with their two children walking up snow-thick STREET. Snow is no longer falling.

The sound of Sunday church bells rises.

And, black for Sunday, people hurry by over the white snow.

106

CITY SQUARE.

Outside Hocking's Academy Mr. and Mrs. Webb stand shivering and waiting, the baby huddled in Mrs. Webb's shawls, the little boy with his hands dug deep in Mr. Webb's coat pocket.

The door of Hocking's Academy opens.

The Policeman comes out.

A Porter stands at the door.

POLICEMAN. If there's a new subject comes in to-day, let
    me know.

He walks towards Rock's Academy, beckoning the Webbs to
    follow him.

He knocks on the door of Rock's Academy.

The grille opens.

From the Policeman's angle we see Tom's face through the bars.

    POLICEMAN'S VOICE. Have you had a new subject to-day?

    TOM. Aye.

    POLICEMAN'S VOICE. Open the door.

The door opens.

The Policeman walks in.

107

SMALL DARK ROOM off the HALL in ROCK'S ACADEMY.

We see the figures of Tom and the Policeman, and the shape of the
    tea-chest.

    POLICEMAN. Open the chest.

Tom opens the tea-chest.

The Policeman looks down into it.

    POLICEMAN. When was it brought?

    TOM. An hour ago.

    POLICEMAN. Who brought it?

CUT to CLOSE-UP of Mrs. Flynn's face. With a sudden
after-death jerk of the muscles, her mouth drops open, as though
she were speaking.

And Tom speaks as the mouth opens.

    TOM'S VOICE. Fallon and Broom.

CUT BACK to the small dark room, the Policeman, and Tom.

    POLICEMAN. Fetch in the old couple. They're waiting
    outside.

Tom goes out.

The Policeman looks round the dark room. We follow his eyes

we see, in a corner, what might be a body covered with a sheet:
in another corner, what might be a cupboard or an upright coffin.

POLICEMAN. [In a whisper.] Cold!

Mr. and Mrs. Webb come into the room.
The Policeman nods towards the open tea-chest.
Timidly they move towards it and look down.

MR. WEBB. The old woman.

Mrs. Webb nods and crosses herself.

POLICEMAN. What was her name?

CUT again to CLOSE-UP of Mrs. Flynn's face.

MRS. WEBB'S VOICE. Mrs. Flynn. . . .

108

REFERENCE LIBRARY IN ROCK'S ACADEMY.

Rock, a sheet of paper in his hand, is walking up and down, in a
characteristic lecture manner, behind his desk.
Some distance away, the other side of the desk, sits Murray.

ROCK. [Gesturing with the paper in his hand.] If this does
not upset some apple-carts, I shall believe that the apples
have been glued on like the coco-nuts in coco-nut shies; if
this does not help to change the idiotic laws that apply to
our profession, I shall run amok; I shall send Doctor
Hocking a Christmas Greeting and sign it 'Yours in
Homage'; I shall place my spiritual welfare in the hands
of the Reverend Doctor Lever and have my seat *reserved*
in hell.

MURRAY. I tell you, this isn't the time to attack.

ROCK. The national anthem of the rabbit world.

MURRAY. If you publish that letter now, attacking the system
by which the medical schools get their bodies, you 'll be
raising a question you might have some difficulty in
answering *yourself*.

ROCK. Am I still a Doctor Bluebeard to you, then, you terrified old lady? Do I spend my nights a-murdering?

MURRAY. I do not know, sir, what you do with your nights. I do not imagine that you can *sleep*. But I do know that *Fallon* and *Broom* are murderers. It is only my respect for you, and my great obligations, and my *cowardice*, that have stopped me from running out of this murder school and telling the whole city what I know and what I guess. . . . Even so, there are rumours. *I* have not spread them. But Jennie's death, and Billy's, have not passed *quite* unnoticed. Rumours are contagious.

ROCK. So are scabies. To destroy them you do not wear the armour of defence, you wield the weapon of sulphur ointment. And, by God, there's sulphur in this letter. . . .

Tom comes in.

TOM. The police have been here.

ROCK. What is yours, sir? A rum and bitters?

TOM. [Bewildered.] Sir?

ROCK. Since you do not knock before you come in, I must assume that this is a public-house. . . .

TOM. I beg your pardon, sir, but the police came about the new subject. Fallon and Broom, sir.

ROCK. Am I never to hear the end of those men's names?

MURRAY. [Softly.] Never, perhaps. . . .

TOM. And they're taking the subject away. . . .

ROCK. Why didn't you call the police? . . .

TOM. [More bewildered.] Sir, I . . .

ROCK. Go away and lock up the silver. If there isn't any silver, lock up Mr. Mattheson: he has a gold tooth.

And Tom goes out.

MURRAY. Must you antagonize every one?

ROCK. Yes.

MURRAY. You heard? The police.

ROCK. Outside the gates of hell are not the words 'Abandon Hope All Ye Who Enter Here,' but 'I Told You So.'

MURRAY. And if the police ask me questions, as they are bound to do, what shall I say?

ROCK. Say nothing. Squeak. They will recognize the voice of a rat.

Murray goes to the door. As he opens it Rock speaks.

ROCK. You will find cheese in the larder. Leave some for Tom.

The door slams.

CLOSE-UP of Rock. The sardonicism, the mockery, have vanished from his face.

DISSOLVE.

109

LONG SHOT of LONG CORRIDOR IN ROCK'S ACADEMY.

We see Tom coming up towards us from the end of the Corridor.

We see him open a door, put his head round the door. We hear him speak into the room behind the door, but are too far away to catch the words.

He comes on up the Corridor, opens another door, puts his head round the door. We hear him speak into the room behind the door, but though his voice is louder now, we still cannot catch the words.

He comes on up the Corridor, opens the door of the Reference Library, puts his head round the door. And now we are close enough to hear the words.

TOM. Fallon and Broom. They've arrested Fallon and Broom. Murder.

He withdraws his head.

From the opposite end of the Corridor we now see, in *LONG SHOT*, Tom padding on, away from camera. . . .

DISSOLVE.

110

To another CORRIDOR.

TRACK UP the empty Corridor.

As we track we hear a mumble of voices growing louder. We reach
a door marked 'Board Room.'

The noise rises.

111

INTERIOR OF BOARD ROOM.

Around the long table are attorneys, counsel, police officials, Hocking, and Green.

> FIRST POLICE OFFICIAL. . . . and if Doctor Rock did not
> know that these bodies were murdered, he's a far less canny
> gentleman than I supposed. . . .

> FIRST ATTORNEY. He knew. One corpse might pass him
> by, but Fallon and Broom were in the wholesale trade. . . .

> SECOND POLICE OFFICIAL. Indict him as accessory after
> the fact. . . .

> HOCKING. I do not exonerate Doctor Rock, but I will not
> have the whole medical profession of the City put on trial.

> GREEN. Accuse Rock, you accuse the integrity of all the
> surgeons in the City.

The Chairman (the Lord Chief Justice) nods in agreement.

> HOCKING. Oh, more than that. The whole aristocracy of
> learning that has been so carefully built up would be
> tumbled to the ground. The stain upon his character
> would spread across the whole of our culture. There could
> be no more respect for us. Indictment of Rock would
> mean *the death of a class.* . . .

112

PRIVATE SMOKEROOM IN AN INN (as in Sequence 27).

The two old gentlemen are seated there with silver tankards in
their hands.

FIRST GENTLEMAN. A great pity his letter appeared in all the newspapers. . . .

SECOND GENTLEMAN. On the very day of the arrest. Your health!

FIRST GENTLEMAN. Health!

SECOND GENTLEMAN. It was so very untactful.

There is a silence during which they drink. They gaze at their tankards.

FIRST GENTLEMAN. 'We must have more bodies,' he said. Dear, dear.

SECOND GENTLEMAN. We must have more *murders*.

FIRST GENTLEMAN. An ugly word, Richard.

SECOND GENTLEMAN. Doctor Rock has endangered the dignity of the higher professions. . . . If he is indicted as accessory after the fact . . .

FIRST GENTLEMAN. No, no, Richard, that must never be. Guilty or not guilty, his part in this affair must be kept in a decent obscurity, or Anarchy will be walking abroad in the land. . . .

SECOND GENTLEMAN. They should all be shot against the wall. . . .

FIRST GENTLEMAN. Who, Richard?

The Second Gentleman makes a vague, sweeping gesture.

SECOND GENTLEMAN. All of 'em. . . .

113

CLOSE SHOT of two elderly professors in mortar-boards and gowns, against the background of a very large, ornately gold-framed portrait of another old professor.

FIRST PROFESSOR. I agree with you entirely. His whole attitude to society spelt ruin from the first. Attack Tradition, it always bites back; and its teeth are well grounded.

SECOND PROFESSOR. A man who could be so persistently and obnoxiously rude to his elders and intellectual betters would think *nothing* of murdering his *own children* for a penny piece.

FIRST PROFESSOR. That is, perhaps, a little extravagant. We *must* disregard personal prejudice, though I agree that to be called 'anaemic buffoon' could not predispose him in your favour. But Rock is a *symbol*. . . .

SECOND PROFESSOR. I agree. A symbol of scholarship. In a manner of speaking, we could regard ourselves as 'the royal family of the intellect,' and . . .

FIRST PROFESSOR. My dear Fraser! . . .

SECOND PROFESSOR. . . . and if a member of the royal family is accused of a commoner's crime, then it is the *whole family* that is accused. An elaborate simile—but you see my point?

And the two professors wag their chins in complete agreement.

114

INTERIOR OF BOARD ROOM.

Around the table the attorneys, counsel, police officials, Hocking, and Green.

FIRST ATTORNEY. Perhaps we are forgetting the murder of children and old women in our concern for our sacred society of autocratic schoolmen. . . .

CHAIRMAN. It is a very grave position. . . .

SECOND POLICE OFFICIAL. Rock is guilty of connivance. . . .

FIRST POLICE OFFICIAL. I am afraid we *will* have to use him as a witness, gentlemen. . . .

CHAIRMAN. Oh, certainly, certainly. . . .

The police officials rise.

CHAIRMAN. [In an undertone to Hocking next to him.] But we won't call him, of course.

115

CORRIDOR IN ROCK'S ACADEMY.

Tom padding up the Corridor.

He stops outside the Reference Library, opens the door.

From behind him we see into the library.

Rock is seated at his desk.

>TOM. Broom has turned king's evidence, sir.
>
>ROCK. [Without looking up.] The king will be pleased. . . .

Tom closes the door, pads on up the long Corridor again, and turns a corner, leaving the Corridor empty.

We hear the very distant noise of a crowd. . . .

116

LONG SHOT of narrow CITY STREET.

Early morning.

The street is empty.

We hear, kept very low, the noise of a great crowd: the grumbling of a sea far off.

117

LONG SHOT of another narrow, empty STREET.

The noise of a great crowd rising, slowly.

118

LONG SHOT of another narrow, empty STREET.

Then, across the far end of the desolate tunnel of the street, we see the crowd surging.

And the noise increases.

The camera moves down the narrow street towards the surge of the crowd and the increasing noise.

It moves past empty doorways.

And out of the empty doorways, through the clamour of the nearing crowd, we hear chanted:

>FIRST VOICE. Up the alley and down the street . . .

On, on, past another doorway.

>SECOND VOICE. Fallon and Broom sell bones and meat. . . .

Past another doorway.

THIRD VOICE. Fallon's the butcher, Broom's the thief . . .

Now we are nearly among the crowd pouring past the narrow street end, but we hear a fourth voice through the noise. . . .

FOURTH VOICE. And Rock's the boy who buys the beef. . . .

And now, through and under the loud noise of the crowd, we hear many voices together taking up the chant.

The camera cranes with and over the heads of the crowd and up to the windows of the court-room, and into the court-room.

119

COURT-ROOM.

We see the backs of the judges.

We move past them, across the court, towards the dock.

As we move we hear the droning voice of the Clerk of the Court. . . .

    CLERK. Robert Fallon and Nelly Connor, you are both and each of you indicted and accused . . .

In the dock, facing us, are Fallon and Nelly. They are both more neatly dressed than usual. Nelly is in black. Fallon is clean-shaven.

We move past them.

Now from behind them, we look down at the Clerk of the Court, who is seated beneath the judges' bench.

The Clerk has not stopped speaking. Now the sound of his voice rises.

    CLERK. . . . that albeit by the laws of this and every other well-governed realm, murder is a crime of an heinous nature, and severely punishable, yet true it is and of verity that you the said Robert Fallon and Nelly Connor are both and each, or one or other of you, guilty of the said crime. . . .

The sound of the Clerk's voice is lowered. Now it is a drone the words of which we cannot catch.

And, through the droning, we hear the muffled noise of the crowd outside.

We move, past Fallon and Nelly, towards the judges.

PAN ALONG the Judges' bench.

PAN DOWN to the Clerk. The Clerk's voice rises.

> CLERK. . . . when she the said Jennie Bailey was lying in the said house in a state of intoxication, and did, by the pressure thereof, and by covering her mouth and nose with your body or person, and forcibly compressing her throat with your hands, and forcibly keeping her down, notwith-standing her resistance, or in some other way to the prosecutor unknown . . .

CUT to *CLOSE-UP* of Fallon.

> CLERK. . . . preventing her from breathing, did suffocate or strangle her. . . .

The noise of the crowd rises, then is dimmed into a background.

DISSOLVE to

120

ROCK'S LECTURE HALL.

Evening.

The background of the crowd noise.

Rock is on the platform.

The candles are lit on the platform table.

The auditorium is crowded with students.

The noise of the crowd rises violently.

Through the noise of the crowd, we hear the percussive voice-beat of 'Rock! Rock! Rock!'

And, like a cymbal clashing, the sharp crash of smashed glass.

Stones hurl through the shattered window at one side of the Lecture Hall.

The students stampede to their feet.

And a heavy stone crashes at Rock's foot.

The students begin to rush down the gallery steps towards the doors
and the platform, shouting.

Rock stands rigid.

He pales with temper, glaring at the rushing students as though they
were his enemies.

In its intensity, his dignity is malevolent.

> ROCK. Gentlemen!

Cold, controlled fury stops the rush.

The students stand frozen.

The noise of the crowd is still loud.

> ROCK. I have attempted to teach you the dignity of man;
> I have succeeded in producing the degradation of a *mob*.
> Because the verminous gutter-snipes of the City snarl and
> gibber in the street, because the scum from the brothels and
> the rot-gut shops howl for blood outside my window, must
> *you* conduct yourselves, in return, as though you were born
> in a quagmire and nurtured on hog-wash?
>
> Take your seats. Pay no attention to *the mob*. The mob
> can never win. Remember that the louder a man shouts,
> the emptier is his argument.
>
> Remember that you are here to study osteology, syndes-
> mology, myology, angiology, neurology, splanchnology:
> not bar-room pugilism or the morals of the crapulous bog-
> trotter and the tosspot.
>
> [In his usual lecturing voice.] The heart, gentlemen, is
> a four-chambered muscular bag which lies in the cavity
> of the thorax . . .

DISSOLVE to

121

CITY STREET.

Night.

The noise of the crowd is a distant, insistent background. We see,
striding in front of us, the black-cloaked top-hatted figure of
Rock with his heavy stick.

We follow him along the street.

Two figures, muffled against the cold, come out of a side-street.

They stumble into Rock.

He pushes them aside.

And suddenly one of them cries out:

> FIRST MAN. Rock! Rock! Doctor Rock!

Rock strides on.

The men cry after him, and follow him down the street, though keeping a safe distance from him.

> SECOND MAN. Doctor Rock! Rock!

And, from some way off, we hear the crowd take up the percussive noise of 'Rock! Rock! Rock!'

122

DISSOLVE to Rock, hatless, but still in his cloak, entering ELIZABETH'S ROOM.

Elizabeth, by the fire, is sewing.

Elizabeth looks up as he comes in, and puts her sewing down.

He crosses to her; kisses her; stands still then, looking down at her.

CLOSE-UP of Rock and Elizabeth.

> ROCK. Oh, there's peace in here.
>
> ELIZABETH. You didn't come home *alone* through the streets? I've been hearing the crowd everywhere, all the evening.
>
> ROCK. Alone.
>
> ELIZABETH. They might have hurt you. . . .
>
> ROCK. Hurt *me*?

With a flourish he opens his cloak. Stuck in a belt around his waist are two pistols and a long dagger.

> ROCK. I'd fell them to the ground. I'd flood the gutters with their . . .

Elizabeth begins to laugh, though quite gently.

> ELIZABETH. Take off your cloak. And put your silly knives and guns away. You're like a boy pretending to be a

highwayman. 'Stand and deliver.' Oh, Thomas, my
dear . . .

He takes off his cloak and flings it over a chair and places the belt,
the knife, and the guns on a table near the fire: a small table
covered with sewing and bales of wool and cotton reels.

ELIZABETH. Why do you have to go out alone at night,
now? Why do you *always* have to be alone?

ROCK. If the crowd wants me, it can have me. I am not
going to hide. I am not going to surround myself by a
company of paid protectors. . . .

ELIZABETH. [Softly.] I've always wanted to see another
country. Couldn't we go away? Every one is against us
here, now.

The distant noise of the crowd.

ELIZABETH. The women in the street didn't nod to me this
morning. Not because I'm your wife—that's why they
used to have nothing to do with me—but because *you*'re
my husband.

ROCK. We won't go away.

ELIZABETH. [Gently, as throughout.] I know why. You
want to show them that they can't hurt you by calling you
names. You want to show them that you don't *mind* when
they say that you told those men to murder people. But
they *do* hurt you.

ROCK. *Time's a wilderness.* [Then, in a changed voice.] Do
you remember walking in the park? Oh, not so long
ago. It was very, very, very cold and windy, people were
scudding along like ships in a gale, and I remember thinking:
'Here's my life going true and even, and my children
growing, and Elizabeth with me for ever, and books to
write, and work to do. . . . Lord, but it's a happy time
. . . even in the unhappy times.

ELIZABETH. I'm with you for ever, that's true. And
there's books to write, and work to do.

Noise of the crowd nearer.

119

ROCK. [Suddenly in another mood.] I was successful, I was established, I was standing in the light. . . . Then out of the mud of the darkness come two ignorant animals, and slowly, quite unknown to themselves, they set about the task of bringing my life and my work down, down, into the slime that bred them. . . . Perhaps from the very moment of their monstrous births, it was decreed, by some sadistic jack-in-office of the universe, that they should befoul and ruin a fellow creature they had never heard of: a garrulous, over-credulous, conceited little anatomist, in a city they had never seen. . . .

From outside the noise of the crowd rises. And as the noise rises, so the voices of Elizabeth and Rock become quieter and more intimate.

ELIZABETH. Let us go away.

ROCK. No, we must stay for ever.

ELIZABETH. I have never asked you before, Thomas, because I love you. Did you know that the bodies that those men brought you had been murdered?

The noise of the crowd rises. Now it is very loud.

And the night sky beyond the window is glowing.

Elizabeth and Rock turn sharply to look towards the window.

VOICES OF THE CROWD. Rock! Rock!
Hang Rock!
Burn him!
Burn!
Burn!
Rock's the boy who buys the beef. . . .

Annabella comes in. She is palely, composedly angry.

ANNABELLA. Do you know what those hooligans are *doing*, Thomas?

She crosses to the window.

ROCK. I gather that they are not subscribing to a testimonial to me. . . .

ANNABELLA. Look! Look!

She points accusingly out of the window.

And Rock and Elizabeth, he with his arm around her shoulder, cross to Annabella's side and look, through the window, down on to the street.

123

STREET OUTSIDE ROCK'S HOUSE.

We see, from the window, the crowd straining against the iron railings of the house; the crowd, in the middle of the street, dancing with torches in their hands; the crowd carrying an effigy of Rock, an absurdly top-hatted scarecrow; the crowd waving their torches, stamping, howling, making a witches' Sabbath in the decorous, graciously façaded street.

And then the effigy, the guy carried on a pole, is held in a position directly opposite the window.

And a young woman with wild hair thrusts her blazing torch into the belly of the effigy.

In the torchlight, in the light of the burning Rock, we see that the young woman is Alice.

And another torch is thrust into the burning body; and another; and another.

Soon the effigy is writhing on fire. And the crowd waves it, crying in a high, hysterical triumph.

And they carry it along the street; and the dark figures of the crowd, their torches above them like long streams of fiery hair, follow it down the street.

124

CITY SQUARE.

Night.

Outside Rock's Academy stand Murray and Tom.

Crowd noise, in the not so far distance.

MURRAY. What's the light over there?

The sky beyond the Square is glowing.

TOM. They're burning an auld scarecrow of the Doctor in the streets.

CLOSE SHOT of Murray. He says, softly:

MURRAY. Can that children's magic bring back the dead?

The crowd noise rises on the wind.

MURRAY. Here we are, Tom, the two of us: the two 'rats'! the two 'deserters'!

TOM. Aye, the Doctor was wrong again. We're no 'rats' or 'deserters.' He should have known we didna want to lose our jobs, eh, Mr. Murray?

Murray draws a little way apart from Tom, then asks abruptly:

MURRAY. What's the time?

TOM. One after midnight. The trial's been nearly twelve hours now. . . .

CLOSE SHOT of Murray.

MURRAY. It took a few short minutes to stop her breath. . . .

125

COURT-ROOM.

Broom in the witness-box.

We see him very close.

We hear the Prosecutor, but do not see him.

PROSECUTOR'S VOICE. What did he do then?

BROOM. He got on her with his breast on her head, and kept in her breath; she gave a kind of cry and moaned a little after the first cry. . . .

CUT to CLOSE-UP of Fallon in the dock.

PROSECUTOR'S VOICE. Did he say anything while this was going on?

BROOM'S VOICE. No, he got up then and put his hand across her mouth and kept it there three or four minutes. She appeared quite dead then.

PROSECUTOR'S VOICE. Were you looking on all this while?

CUT to *CLOSE-UP* of Broom.

> BROOM. I was sittin' on the chair.
> PROSECUTOR'S VOICE. Did you sit in that chair and see
> Fallon for ten minutes killing the woman, and offer her no
> assistance?
> BROOM. Aye.

Broom smiles.

126

NEWSPAPER OFFICE.

Crowd noise from outside.

A room with a long, large window.

The First Reporter is writing at a table.

The Second Reporter is walking up and down the room and
glancing, every few moments, out of the window.

> SECOND REPORTER. Was he smiling when he said *that*?
> FIRST REPORTER. [Without looking up.] If you call it
> smiling.
> SECOND REPORTER. What did he look like?
> FIRST REPORTER. [Briefly, as he writes.] Devil.
> SECOND REPORTER. Fallon?
> FIRST REPORTER. Quite quiet. Vurry polite.
> SECOND REPORTER. And the woman?
> FIRST REPORTER. Sober.

The crowd noise rises.

> SECOND REPORTER. What are you calling the article? [At
> the window.] They're running down the street now. . .
> Thousands of them. . . .
> FIRST REPORTER. 'Justice.'
> SECOND REPORTER. 'Broom! Broom! Broom!' . . . D' you
> hear them?
> FIRST REPORTER. Broom 'll go free.
> SECOND REPORTER. [Still looking out of the window.]

There s another fire over Newington way . . . somewhere near Rock's place. . . . D' you hear them?

FIRST REPORTER. [Writing, not looking up.] They won't call Rock as a witness. That'll be taken care of. . . .

A great cry from the crowd outside. . . .

SECOND REPORTER. D' you hear that? . . .

FIRST REPORTER. I 'm not deaf. They 're nearing the end now. . . .

127

COURT-ROOM.

CLOSE SHOT of Lord Meadowbank. Camera *PANS ALONG* judges' faces.

LORD MEADOWBANK. My Lords, I am confident that, although speaking in the presence of your Lordships, so much better instructed than myself, and so able to correct me were I in error, there is no chance of my being contra-dicted when I say that in the history of this country—nay, in the whole history of civilized society—there has never been exhibited such a system of barbarous and savage iniquity, or anything at all corresponding in atrocity, to what this trial has brought to light. . . .

128

NEWSPAPER OFFICE.

Night.

The two reporters.

The First Reporter flings down his pen.

FIRST REPORTER. Fallon guilty. The rest—innocent! And my title is '*Justice.*' I wrote the verdict *myself*, hours ago. Only the sentence now: I 've written that, too.

COURT-ROOM.

> LORD CHIEF JUSTICE. The Lord Justice Clerk and Lord
> Commissioners of Justiciary in respect of the verdict before
> recorded, determine and adjudge the said Robert Fallon,
> to be carried from the bar, and to be fed upon bread
> and water only until Wednesday, the 28th January, and
> upon that day to be taken forth to the common place of
> execution and then and there between the hours of eight
> and ten o'clock to be hanged by the neck until he be
> dead. And may Almighty God have mercy on your soul.

DISSOLVE to

130

Large *CLOSE-UP* of Rock.

> ROCK. I have no need of your sympathy. When I see a
> tear, I smell a crocodile.

TRACK BACK to show that Rock is standing on the platform
of the empty Lecture Hall. Murray, a good distance from Rock,
stands at the window, looking out.

Their voices echo in the Hall.

> MURRAY. [Turning round.] For God's sake, Thomas, can
> you do nothing but—stand still and gibe?
> ROCK. Would you have me death-dance and *moan*, like a
> Gaelic dipsomaniac at a distillery fire? Must tragedy go
> immediately to the feet and the tongue? Because I can
> observe my history *calmly* as it burns and topples around
> me, you emotional gluttons think yourselves cheated. 'Oh,
> he can't *feel* anything,' you say. 'When we told him his
> life was over, he did not tear the relics of his hair or address
> the travelling moon in blank verse. He blew his nose and
> called for Burgundy.'
> MURRAY. [Deliberately.] Fallon is to hang.
> ROCK. A quick end. If they wished his death to be longer

and infinitely more painful, they should marry him to Doctor Hocking's daughter.

MURRAY. Fallon is to hang. Nelly Connor is 'not guilty'! Broom and his woman are free to murder again! And *you*?

ROCK. I shall stay here.

I shall listen to the voices of the crowd outside my window, *inside my head*; it will not be long before they forget me; I shall never forget them.

I shall stay here. The whispers of the slanderer and the backbiter will always be with me: mice behind the wall.

I shall stay here. I shall count my friends on the fingers of one hand, then on one finger, then on none.

Camera Cranes Back, looking down at Rock and Murray all the time, over the empty tiers of the classroom.

Although Rock becomes further and further off, in *LONG SHOT*, the sound, booming hollowly through the empty classroom, remains in full close-up.

ROCK. My lectures will be very well attended, at the beginning. I shall possess a sinister attraction to the young: dangerous and exciting, like dining with a vampire. But the attendance will diminish.

I shall stay here to see in the eyes of the passing stranger in the street cruelty and contempt; in the eyes of the poor the terrible accusation: 'You killed the lost, the weak, the homeless, the hopeless, the helpless. Murderer of the poor!'

God help me, life will go on. . . .

131

CONDEMNED CELL.

Fallon on a chair in the middle of the cell.

His hair is shaven.

A Phrenologist is measuring his head. He speaks the measurements aloud to an assistant, who writes them down in a book.

Fallon submits, with interest, to the examination.

PHRENOLOGIST. From the ear to lower Individuality: 5 inches. From the ear to the centre of philo-progenitiveness: 4.8. From the ear to Benevolence: 5.7. From the ear to Destructiveness: 6.125.

Let us see:

Acquisitiveness: large.

Secretiveness: large.

Wit: deficient.

Cautiousness: h'm, rather large.

Sense of Tune: moderate.

Self-esteem: rather large.

Hope: small.

132

EXTERIOR OF PRISON.

Night.

A coach draws up.

The driver is heavily shawled about, and his hat is pulled down over his eyes.

And two cloaked, muffled figures hurry Broom towards the coach.

Broom is wrapped in a thick coat, and hooded. It is hard to recognize him.

But suddenly, at the door of the coach, he pulls back his hood, looks up at the sky.

He shakes his shaven head, like a monstrous dog coming out of the water.

And he begins to laugh his high, clear, yelping laugh as the two cloaked figures smuggle him into the coach.

The coach moves off, out of picture.

133

MARKET-PLACE.

Late evening.

The stalls closed down.

And a woman's scream, a scream of hate and anger, is coming from a Market tavern.

And with her scream are mingled the voices of men and women: voices shouting, cursing, and threatening.

Then a knot of people tangles inside the open door of the tavern.

A whirl of arms and a squall of voices.

And we see Kate thrown out of the tavern on to the cobble stones of the Market.

She stumbles to her feet, runs, squawking like a chased hen, down the Market.

But only the voices chase her.

People pour from the tavern, stand outside it, throw stones after her, manure, rubbish.

Kate runs on, huddled.

And windows, high up in the tenements around the Market, open.

And the contents of buckets are thrown upon her as she runs.

134

ROAD ON THE OUTSKIRTS OF THE CITY.

Night.

The road is long and winding.

We see Nelly Connor, with a bundle on her back, coming towards us, along the road, out of the distance.

She is pushing a hurly: a hurly with old boots upon it, and remnants of clothing, and odds and ends from the room in Rag-and-Bone Alley, and shapes one cannot identify in the night.

And we hear her voice as she pushes her barrow through darkness up the desolate road that leads out of the City.

> NELLY's VOICE. [Softly.]
> Old boots to sell! . . . Cat-skin! . . . *Human hair!* . . .

NEWSPAPER OFFICE.

Daylight.

We see the street through the tall window.

The Second Reporter stands at the window, looking out, his back towards us.

The First Reporter sits at the other side of the window, a pad on his knee. Through the window we see, at the end of the street, in *LONG SHOT*, a scaffold.

The platform of the scaffold is raised above the heads of the crowd.

On the platform we see the gibbet; it is shaped like a T with one additional vertical on the right.

On the platform are several figures: clergymen, magistrates, hangman, and Fallon.

And we hear the crowd noise rise.

And looking through the window at the scene of execution, and hearing the cries of the crowd, we hear, too, the voices of the two men at the window.

> SECOND REPORTER. Do you hear?
> 'Hang Broom! Hang Rock!'
> FIRST REPORTER. Fallon's on his knees. He's praying.

The noise of the crowd rises. Then:

> SECOND REPORTER. The rope's round his neck. They've put a cotton nightcap on his head.
> FIRST REPORTER. Good night.

The noise of the crowd rises again.

> CRIES OF THE CROWD. You'll see Billy Bedlam in a minute.
> FIRST REPORTER. What are they shouting?
> SECOND REPORTER. 'You'll see Billy Bedlam in a minute!'
> He's on the drop.

A great cheer from the crowd.

> FIRST REPORTER. He was always one for dancing. He's dancing now.

136

CLOSE SHOT of Alice and Murray at a table in a TAVERN.

Around them the noise of the Market-place drinking. And pipes in the distance.

> ALICE. Fallon's dead—why isn't the Doctor dead? Nobody remembers Jennie now.
>
> MURRAY. Oh, there's lots of ways of dying. *I* remember.

137

CLOSE SHOT of Annabella and Elizabeth; behind them, the window of ELIZABETH'S ROOM looking out on the wintry trees in the garden.

> ANNABELLA. Do you *know* what it is to be lonely? I've always been lonely. I wanted to be mistress of my brother's house, I wanted to give dinner parties and dances and be charming and admired. I wanted to marry. But people wouldn't visit us because *you* married *him*. It doesn't matter now. Now nobody'll come. . . .
>
> ELIZABETH. I married him because I loved him. But we're only a very little part of his life, Bella.
>
> I've been lonely, too.

138

CLOSE SHOT of Hocking and the Chairman (the Lord Chief Justice, whom we saw in Sequences 111 and 114) against the background of imposing bookcases.

> CHAIRMAN. So, officially speaking, he's innocent as a lamb, the wolf.
>
> HOCKING. We saved him from a criminal prosecution.
>
> CHAIRMAN. Of course, of course. In order to save the good name of society. Fallon and Broom could have brought

their bodies to *you*, of course. It just happened it was
Rock they chose.

HOCKING. I would have none of their bodies.

CHAIRMAN. No?

HOCKING. But now it's all over. All over. We can speak
our minds now.

CHAIRMAN. We save him from public ruin, so that we can
ruin him privately. H'm, I'm sure he's grateful. . . .

139

LECTURE HALL OF ROCK'S ACADEMY.

Rock is on the platform.

The auditorium is densely packed.

We see Rock from the back of the Hall, over the heads of the
students.

And we move, slowly, over the heads towards him as he speaks.

ROCK. To think, then, is to enter into a perilous country,
colder of welcome than the polar wastes, darker than a
Scottish Sunday, where the hand of the unthinker is always
raised against you, where the wild animals, who go by such
names as Envy, Hypocrisy, and Tradition, are notoriously
carnivorous, and *where the parasites rule.*

To *think* is dangerous. The majority of men have found
it easier to writhe their way into the parasitical bureaucracy,
or to *droop* into the slack ranks of the ruled. I beg you all
to devote your lives to danger; I pledge you to adventure;
I command you to experiment. [Slowly.] Remember that
the practice of Anatomy is absolutely vital to the *progress* of
medicine. Remember that the progress of medicine is vital
to the progress of mankind. And mankind is worth
fighting for: killing and lying and dying for. Forget
what you like. Forget all I have ever told you. But
remember that. . . .

Now we see Rock in *CLOSE-UP*.

CITY STREET.

Gathering dusk.

We hear the thin, high singing of the wind in the street.

And, in the background, the sound of the voices of children drifting through the dusk.

Rock, from a grey distance, is walking towards us along the street. He is cloaked, top-hatted.

And as he comes closer to us a little girl runs out of the shadows of a side-street, runs barefoot through the wind, her black hair leaping.

She is grimed from the gutters of the city; her dress is thin and ragged; one shoulder is naked.

And she runs at Rock's side, crying out:

> GIRL. Give us a penny, mister, give us a penny. . . .

The camera *TRACKS BACK* as Rock, and the little girl running at his side, move on down the street.

Then Rock stops, at a corner.

And the little girl stops; she stands still in a shadow at the mouth of a narrow tunnel-like street. She is almost lost in the shadow, her hair is mixed into the darkness, but we see her white face and white, naked shoulder.

Rock stands just outside the shadow.

He puts a penny in her hand.

He looks down at her, and is silent for a moment.

> ROCK. It's a bitter cold night to be running about in the streets. You should go home.

The child in the shadows shakes her head.

> CHILD. Granny says I can't come home till I got four-pence. . . .

Rock fumbles in his pocket for another coin.

The child holds out her hand from the shadow around her.

ROCK. What's your name, lassie?

CHILD. I'm Maggie Bell.

ROCK. [Almost as though to himself.] I'm Doctor Rock.

And the child runs screaming into the darkness.

And Rock walks on, away from us.

141

HILL ABOVE THE CITY.

The dusk is deeper. . . .

The wind is blowing wilder. . . .

We look down the hill.

Out of the dusk, a long way off, Rock is climbing up towards us.

And as he climbs, we hear his voice. But it is only the little, wind-blown whisper of a voice, and we cannot hear a word of it.

And as he climbs on and up, so the windy whisper loudens and we begin to hear the words.

We begin to hear the fragments of sentences.

We hear some words and then the wind rises for a second and blows them away.

Then we hear more words, from the voice of his mind; the wind again will not let the words finish but blows them away.

And again; and again; and again.

Always the voice is the voice of Rock, but it is never twice on the same level: it is the voice of Rock young, then old, then gay, then sad; a high voice, a low voice.

And the sound of it rises as he climbs.

> ROCK'S VOICE. And the child in the cold runs away from my name. . . .
>
> My name is a ghost to frighten children. . . .
>
> Will *my* children cry 'Murder' and 'Blood' when I touch them . . . as if my hands were Fallon's hands? . . .
>
> 'Be good, be good, or the terrible Doctor will come with his knife.'

133

Poor Billy! I came to you with my knife.

Did I *know*, did I *know* from the very beginning?

Never answer, never answer, even to yourself alone in the night. . . .

All 's over now. . . .

Oh, Elizabeth, hold my hand. . . .

'Oh, it isn't a hand, it 's a pair of scissors! . . .'

Did I set myself up as a little god over death?

Over death. . . .

All over . . . over . . . over . . .

Did I set myself above pity? . . .

Oh, my God, I knew what I was doing!

And he passes us and climbs up the long hill, and his voice climbs with him into darkness, into a whisper, into silence, into the climax of .

MUSIC.

THE STORY OF THE FILM

BY DONALD TAYLOR

Since the film has attained a certain intellectual maturity in the half-century since its birth, the publication of screenplays has become increasingly frequent. Hitherto those screenplays which achieve the dignity of print have been verbal transcriptions taken from the finished film, when that film has been successful in the cinemas. It is what is known in the film industry as a 'release script.'

It is worth recording that in the majority of cases, the finished film is very different from the original screenplay as delivered by the script writer. It would be infinitely more instructive to the layman were there to be a comparative publication of the original screenplay alongside a transcription of the finished product. The transcription method does not reveal the essential factor about film-making, which is the varied contributions made by many hands and the constant polishing and alteration that is the integral part of the work.

Even the great Eisenstein was not above attempting to demonstrate his creative competence by publishing graphs of sequences from his films to prove his creative planning; which to the film technician are only too evidently the result of trial and error.

The screenplay of *The Doctor and the Devils* is the first to be published as a book before the film has been produced. This is no doubt due to the literary quality, unusual in this medium. It will be instructive to compare the finished film, when it is produced, with this screenplay.

The most satisfying and commercially successful films have a background of idea which is the driving force behind the plot. The classic example is D. W. Griffith's *Intolerance*. It is insufficient in making any film to have a good plot, if there is no basic motive behind it.

The screenplay of *The Doctor and the Devils* was written because I had been searching for some years to find a story that would pose the question of 'the ends justifying the means.'

Concurrently with this, I had been much interested in James Bridie's play *The Anatomist*. This prompted me to do some research into the character of Dr. Knox, the Edinburgh anatomist of the early nineteenth century. The question of whether he was aware that the bodies supplied to him by two Irish labourers Burke and Hare, for anatomical research and demonstration, were the product of mass murder, seemed to me an interesting basis to illustrate my theme. Contemporary and historical records seemed to assume a verdict of not proven; although Professor Wilson, the brilliant and caustic Edinburgh philosopher, declared in his *Noctes Ambrosianae* that Knox should have been hanged with Burke and Hare. We found such a wealth of material about Dr. Knox that, for all of us who worked on the subject, the study of the man became all absorbing. From this material I organized and wrote a coherent story and commissioned Dylan Thomas, who was then working for me, to write a screen play.

It is surely time that a considered biography was written about Knox, who contributed so much to British anatomical science and was known in his time as a great European figure. The only biography, published in 1870 and never reprinted, was written by his senior demonstrator, who subsequently became Surgeon Extraordinary to Queen Victoria. It is a testament to Dr. Knox's ability as scientist, anatomist, and lecturer, that his chief pupil should have written so glowing a biography thirty years after his death.

The limitations of the film medium are such that one must express a character through a very short series of incidents and these must form a fairly rigid pattern. This means that much that is interesting and significant has to be ruthlessly cut out. For instance, by one of those historical coincidences which seems incredible, Knox was a doctor at Waterloo when Burke, who was subsequently to change the whole pattern of his life, acted as medical orderly in the same battle.

What is in this script is in fact true, although to achieve dramatic construction many of the incidents have had to be telescoped and concentrated. The names of the characters have been changed to

136

conform with film censorship. The only 'invented' individual, who did in fact exist but invented in the sense of character, is the wife of Knox. His biographer makes only two references to her, both of which are significant. At one point he says that Knox 'married beneath him' and the second that 'when she died, he threw himself upon her grave and lay there for hours together.' These two facts made possible a character of charm in a gloomy picture.

Dr. Knox was an odd and eccentric being; he was a man of insignificant height, bald, and with one eye. At the height of his success his anatomical lectures drew not only all the students from the university, but famous people from all over Europe. He was always overdressed and in the height of fashion; the amount of jewellery he wore caused remark among his contemporaries. But he had only to walk in front of his audience to hold them completely under his sway for two or three hours at a time. His lectures, although inspired by an anatomical text, ranged through the whole world of philosophy, art, and manners. He was a man of such diverse attainments that it is hard to conceive that he could ever have achieved so much in the relatively short period when he was famous.

He was at Waterloo as a newly qualified doctor; he was a pioneer and road builder in the development of the Boer States, with such success that he was invited by the Boers to become a member of their legislative assembly; he sat under Cuvier and was much respected by him; he contributed a scientific approach to ethnographical study; he was an indefatigable fisherman and discovered a new species of fish that inhabited Loch Maben; he was a continuous correspondent to every medical journal of his time, and he was a confirmed and distinguished controversialist in newspapers and literary reviews; he contributed much to scientific study and speculation outside his own specialized work in anatomy.

It is a sad fact that so remarkable a man is only remembered to-day because his name is linked with two murderers. This trial ruined his Edinburgh career.

It is ironic that the present acts of Parliament which secure the supply of bodies for anatomical study, should have resulted from the trial of Burke and Hare. Knox was never brought to trial, because the Edinburgh aristocracy of intellect considered that were he to be prosecuted, the intellectual leadership of Scotland that had been so effectively built up to replace the aristocratic leadership destroyed by the rising of '45, could not survive the public arraignment of one of their members.

After the trial of Burke and Hare, Knox was ostracized by Edinburgh society; in the heat of the moment after the trial he was in daily danger of his life from the mob. Although he tried to brave it out, he had eventually to leave Edinburgh, and his detractors claimed that he was last seen lecturing in a circus in Leicester Square, London. The real fact is that ethnography, his abiding passion, led him to lecture to invited audiences, using for demonstration purposes a group of North American Indians who were appearing in a circus.

Although he had many a brush with poverty in his later years, he achieved some measure of security and fame in London. He remained to the end a vigorous correspondent and controversialist, and, whatever Edinburgh society might think, the medical world of London respected him sufficiently to appoint him the first surgeon to the new London Fever Hospital.

I must acknowledge contributions made by members of my film unit, the Strand Film Company, and I must record my grateful thanks to Mr. Earl St. John and the J. Arthur Rank organization for allowing me to publish this work.

D. T.

1953.